SO-AZL-078

Creating

Garden Accents

Step-by-step instructions for 22 projects

this book has been
Donated

in
Loving
Memory
of

Candace Lyn Johnson

By Jerri Farris
Designed by Tim Himsel

CREATIVE
PUBLISHING
international

MINNETONKA, MINNESOTA

Executive Editor: Bryan Trandem
Editorial Director: Jerri Farris
Creative Director: Tim Himsel
Managing Editor: Michelle Skudlarek

Author: Jerri Farris
Designer: Tim Himsel
Editor: Barbara Harold
Project Manager: Tracy Stanley
Copy Editor: Tracy Stanley
Art Director: Russ Kuepper
Tech Art Designer: Jon Simpson
Technical Photo Stylist: Julie Caruso

Photographers: Kim Bailey, Tate Carlson, Andrea Rugg, Joel Schnell
Shop Supervisor: Dan Widerski
Scene Shop Carpenters: Scott Ashfield, Paul Gorton

Director, Production Services: Kim Gerber
Illustrator: Dan Lotts

President/CEO: Michael Eleftheriou
Vice President/Publisher: Linda Ball
Vice President/Retail Sales & Marketing: Kevin Haas

Copyright© 2002
Creative Publishing international, Inc.
5900 Green Oak Drive
Minnetonka, MN 55343
www.creativepub.com
1-800-328-3895
All rights reserved.

Printed by R. R. Donnelley & Sons Co.
10 9 8 7 6 5 4 3 2 1

CREATING GARDEN ACCENTS
Created by: The Editors of Creative
Publishing international, Inc.

Library of Congress Cataloging-in-Publication Data

Farris, Jerri
    Creating garden accents : step-by-step instructions for 22 projects / by Jerri Farris ;
    designed by Tim Himsel.
        p. cm.
    ISBN: 1-58923-041-8 (soft cover)
    1. Garden ornaments and furniture--Design and construction--Amateurs' manuals. I.
    Himsel, Tim. II. Title.

SB473.5.F27 2002
684.1'8--dc21
                                                    2002017352

Contents

Welcome

Gardens are like people: Each is unique. Just as siblings are individuals despite having the same parents, each garden has its own personality, even if it has exactly the same plantings as the one next door. Variations in site, soil, terrain, and orientation create some differences, but the biggest influences on a garden are the personalities and interests of the people who tend it.

Because I knew very little about gardening and almost nothing about plant selection when I established my first perennial bed, I ordered one of those all-you-add-is-water perennial collections from a catalog. In the beginning, the bed was very much like any other established with that collection. But over time, favorites were encouraged to spread while others were restricted; struggling plants were relocated and new species added. Those first plantings evolved into a garden—my garden.

Eventually I began to design and build ornaments and accents for my garden. After a time, a cedar bench rested under the crabapple tree; a copper trellis supported a climbing rose; elaborate plant stakes embraced top-heavy lilies, and turtles rested on posts in beds and borders. As the garden took shape, I began to develop books on the subject. For a woman who started out wary of circular saws and skeptical about propane torches, it's been a remarkable journey.

Tim Himsel, my friend and creative partner, has been my guide, mentor, teacher, and inspiration throughout. He really is a creative genius and mechanical whiz who can coax materials—particularly wire and copper pipe—into practically any shape. As a team, we've now produced five books (including two on garden ornaments and accents), but he still surprises me with his clever solutions to design challenges. Tim's special talent is working out simple processes that anyone can master, even me.

Within the pages that follow, you'll find what we believe is some of our best work ever—projects and ideas that you can bring to life in your own garden. As you begin, we encourage you to adapt, alter, and modify our designs to make them your very own. Experiment. Get creative. And above all, have fun.

Deni Farris

Water Features

There's nothing quite as soothing as the sight and sound of water. Most of us will never live beside the ocean or on the banks of a river, but we still can live with the renewing, comforting presence of water. From the simple birdbath to the more ambitious millstone fountain for a garden pond, the projects in this chapter will help you bring the music and magic of water into your garden.

Water features, such as fountains and copper sprinklers, have become enormously popular in recent years. Garden centers and home stores are filled with items of every shape, style, and price range. Often, I find that the more affordable versions are not very attractive, and the more desirable ones are prohibitively expensive. You can avoid both extremes by making your own water feature from inexpensive but high-quality materials. You can build a copper sprinkler for under $40, or a ground-level fountain for around $100.

Every water feature benefits from regular maintenance. Birds avoid dirty birdbaths and fountains, but mosquitoes and algae love them. Unless you find green slime attractive, plan on cleaning your birdbaths once a week and your fountains twice a month. (You'll find additional information on page 19.)

Yin/Yang Fountain

This simple wash tub fountain creatively uses common materials to create a stylish focal point for any yard or garden. Colored glass accent marbles—arranged in a yin/yang pattern here—perfectly complement the metallic sheen of the galvanized wash tub. The gentle spray of water from a submersible pump adds a soothing effect that makes this fountain a spectacular sight.

Installation of a wash tub fountain can be completed in a single afternoon. Most of the materials can be purchased at a home building center, while the 9-gauge ¾" expanded aluminum grate can be found at a steel yard. The expanded aluminum grate provides a solid bed for the accent marbles, and also protects children and animals from harm.

The pattern for the yin/yang symbol provided on page 108 can be enlarged on a photocopier and used as a template. Or you can create a design of your own to personalize your fountain.

When determining a location for the fountain, make sure there is a GFCI receptacle nearby, or install a new one in a convenient location. After the wash tub fountain is installed, place plants and stones around the edges of the wash tub to disguise the electrical cord as it exits the basin and runs toward the nearest GFCI receptacle.

TOOLS & MATERIALS

- Drill with ¼" (6.35 mm) bit
- ½" (12.7 mm) hole saw
- Caulk gun
- Permanent marker
- Jig saw & metal-cutting blade
- Duct tape
- Shovel
- Tape measure
- Hand tamp
- Level
- Grease pencil
- Scissors
- Galvanized wash tub
- Angle irons (4)

- ½" (12.7 mm) watertight electrical box bushing
- ¼ × ½" (6.35 × 12.7 mm) hex bolts & nuts (8 of each)
- Silicone caulk
- Sand
- 9-gauge (3.75 mm) ¾" (19.05 mm) expanded aluminum grate
- Bricks (2)
- Fountain water pump
- Bell spout
- Landscape fabric
- Black and white glass accent marbles

HOW TO BUILD A YIN/YANG FOUNTAIN

Step A: Prepare the Wash Tub

1. Mark the location for four angle irons around the perimeter of the wash tub, 2" (5 cm) below the rim. Drill pairs of ¼" holes at each location, matching the hole spacing on the angle irons.

2. Fasten an angle iron on the inside of the wash tub at each location, using ¼ × ½" hex bolts with nuts.

3. Drill an exit hole for the water pump cord, 6" (15.25 cm) below the rim, using a ½" hole saw. Install a ½" watertight electrical box bushing in the hole, then run a caulk bead around edges of the bushing.

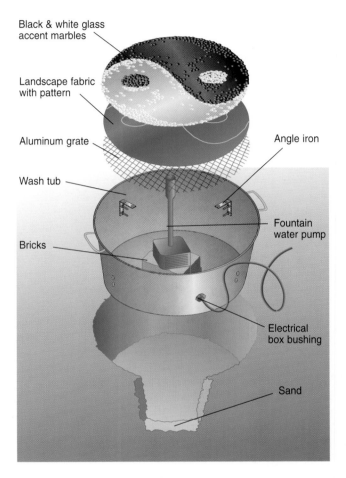

Black & white glass accent marbles

Landscape fabric with pattern

Aluminum grate

Wash tub

Bricks

Angle iron

Fountain water pump

Electrical box bushing

Sand

A. *Drill four pairs of holes in the wash tub and bolt angle irons 2" below the rim, around the perimeter of the tub.*

B. *Cut the expanded metal grate to fit within the tub, then enlarge a hole in the center for the water delivery tube, using a jig saw.*

Step B: Install the Grate

1. Place the wash tub upside down on top of the expanded aluminum grate. Trace the outline of the rim on the grate, using a permanent marker.

2. Use a jig saw with a metal cutting blade to cut the grate ½" inside the rim outline, so the grate will fit within the tub. NOTE: Line the base of the jig saw with duct tape to prevent the surface from being scratched or damaged.

3. Mark the center of the grate and cut a hole large enough for the water delivery tube of the water pump, using a jig saw.

Step C: Install the Wash Tub

1. Dig a hole that is 3" (7.62 cm) shallower than the depth of the wash tub and 2 to 3" (5 to 7.62 cm) wider than its diameter.

2. Add a 3" layer of sand to the hole. Dampen and tamp the sand, then position and level the wash tub, adding sand as necessary, until the top of the tub is 6" above ground level.

3. Position the tub so the exit hole for the water pump electrical cord is facing in the direction of the nearest GFCI receptacle. Backfill around the sides of the wash tub with black dirt to hold the tub in place.

Step D: Install the Water Pump

1. Clean out any sand or dirt, and then put two clean bricks on the bottom of the wash tub.

2. Center the pump on top of the bricks, then thread the water pump electrical cord through the hole in the side of the tub and out to the nearest GFCI receptacle. Caulk around the cord and bushing to create a watertight seal.

3. Place the expanded aluminum grate in the wash tub so that the water delivery tube fits cleanly through the center hole in the grate.

4. Add the bell spout to the water delivery tube, following manufacturer's instructions.

5. Fill the wash tub with water. Turn on the pump and adjust the flow valve, following manufacturer's instructions. Test and adjust the spray pattern until you find one that appeals to you.

Step E: Create the Pattern

1. Remove the grate and trace its outline and the hole for the water delivery pipe onto a piece of landscape fabric. Cut the fabric to fit on top of the grate.

2. Draw the yin/yang symbol—or other design of your choice—onto the top of the fabric with grease pencil. Use a photocopier to enlarge the pattern on page 108 to use as a template.

3. Return the grate to its position in the wash tub and place the landscape fabric over it. Arrange fabric so the symbol is in the position you prefer.

Step F: Arrange the Stones

1. Arrange black and white glass accent marbles on top of the landscape fabric, following the pattern.

2. Place plants and stones at the edge of the fountain to disguise the electrical cord as it exits the wash tub and runs toward the nearest GFCI receptacle.

C. *Dig the hole for the tub, then add a 3" layer of sand. Position and level the tub in the hole, so the top of the tub is 6" above the ground. Fill around edges with black dirt.*

D. *Set the water pump on bricks in the tub, and put the grate in place. Attach the bell spout according to the manufacturer's instructions.*

E. *Cut landscape fabric to fit on top of the grate, then draw a yin/yang symbol on the fabric. Position the fabric in the tub, over the grate.*

F. *Set black and white glass accent marbles on top of the landscape fabric, following the yin/yang pattern.*

VARIATION: PERSONALIZED PATTERN

Decorating a wash tub fountain may be the most satisfying part of the project. Glass accent marbles are available in many colors. Use them to create specific designs or mix them together to add random splashes of color. Use different materials, such as polished stones (left), to add texture and contrast. Decorative grates or copper ornaments (right) can also be used.

Copper Sprinkler

One of the most popular projects we've ever developed is the copper sprinkler from *Building Garden Ornaments*, so we felt obligated to include a sprinkler in this book. The new version combines the simple but ingenious mechanisms from the earlier one with an entirely new head shape and design.

The swivel mechanism incorporates parts from some unexpected sources, but they're all widely available. Copper pipe and fittings are available at virtually any home center. The round brass tubing (made by K&S Engineering) is sold at many hardware stores as well as hobby and crafts centers. The hinge-pin bushings (manufactured by Motormite) are available at many auto parts stores.

The spacing of the holes on this square head is critical, but quite simple. On the sides of the head, the holes face in opposite directions, which creates the directional force that makes the head spin. As water is pushed out the holes, the pressure rotates the head. The holes on each side need to be centered on the pipe. There are holes in the top as well, but they're merely decorative—they play no part in the sprinkler's action.

Unlike many of our copper projects, this one must have watertight solder joints. That means the soldering involved here is a little more delicate than in some of our other projects, but if you work slowly and carefully, it won't be difficult. If necessary, review the soldering techniques described on pages 104 to 105.

TOOLS & MATERIALS

- Tubing cutter
- Wire cutters
- Center punch
- Bench grinder or rotary tool
- Propane torch
- Drill with ¹⁄₁₆" (1.6 mm) twist bit
- Clamp
- Markers, black and red
- ½" (12.7 mm) Type L copper pipe
- ¹¹⁄₃₂" (8.7 mm) brass tubing
- ⁵⁄₁₆" (8 mm) brass tubing
- Wire brush or emery cloth
- Hinge pin bushings (4)
- Solder
- Flux and flux brush
- Pliers

- ½" (12.7 mm) copper tee
- ½" (12.7 mm) copper 90° elbows (4)
- ¼" (6.35 mm) copper tubing (39" [99 cm])
- 1-gallon (4-l) paint can
- 1-quart (1-l) paint can
- Flat washers (4 or 5)
- 10-gauge (3-mm) copper wire (65" [165 cm])
- ½" (12.7 mm) brass shower ell
- 6" (15.25 cm) galvanized wicket
- Machine screws and nuts (2)
- Spray paint, copper color
- ½" (12.7 mm) threaded copper adapter
- Teflon tape
- Hose connector

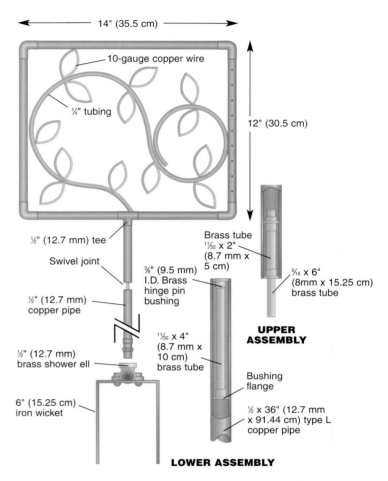

HOW TO BUILD A COPPER SPRINKLER
Step A: Make the Assemblies for the Swivel Joint

1. Cut one 5" (12.7 cm) piece and one 36" (91.44 cm) piece of ½" copper pipe, using a tubing cutter. Also cut one 2" (5 cm) and one 4" (10 cm) piece of ¹¹⁄₃₂" brass tubing, and one 6" (15.25 cm) piece of ⁵⁄₁₆" brass tubing. Deburr the pieces, being careful not to flare the ends; use a wire brush or emery cloth to polish the ends.

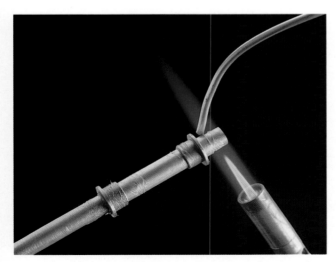

A. *Solder the upper assembly, connecting the ⁵⁄₁₆" tube, the ¹¹⁄₃₂" tube, and the bushing. Heat all three pieces; first feed solder into the joint between the brass tubes, then into the bushing joint.*

2. Test-fit the hinge-pin bushings inside the 5" piece of copper. If necessary, use a bench grinder or a rotary tool to slightly shape the flanges of the hinge pin bushings so they fit snugly within the pipe. Note: To help you create a uniform edge, use a scrap of the ¹¹⁄₃₂" tubing as a spindle.

3. To form the upper assembly, slide a bushing onto each end of the 2" length of ¹¹⁄₃₂" brass tubing, with the flanges facing the ends of the tube. Set the flange of one bushing back ⅛" (3 mm) from the end of the tube. Position the other bushing flush with the opposite end. Slide the 6" length of ⁵⁄₁₆" brass tubing inside the ¹¹⁄₃₂" tube, positioning the inner tube to protrude ⅜" (9.5 mm) beyond the top (set back) bushing.

4. To form the lower assembly, slide a bushing onto each end of the 4" piece of ¹¹⁄₃₂" brass tubing, flanges facing outward, flush with the ends of the tube.

5. Begin soldering at the top of the upper assembly (see pages 104 to 105 for soldering techniques). Heat all three pieces—the ⅜₆" tube, the 1½₂" tube, and the bushing. Feed solder into the joint between the two brass tubes first. Next, feed solder into the bushing joint, approaching that joint from the side opposite the flange.

6. Solder the three remaining bushing joints, each time feeding the solder into the joint from the side opposite the flange.

Step B: Construct the Swivel Joint

1. Flux the inside of the 5" piece of ½" copper and the flange of the bushing on the upper assembly. Slide the assembly inside the copper pipe, positioning the lower bushing to be flush with the end of the copper pipe.

B. *Place the upper and lower assemblies of the swivel joint at the edge of a work surface and solder the joints. Feed the solder from the bottom so the solder doesn't run into the brass tubes.*

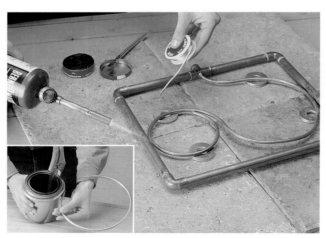

C. *Dry-fit and then solder the rectangle that forms the head. Shape ¼" tubing for the vine (inset), and solder it in place.*

2. Flux the inside of the 36" piece of copper and the shoulder of one bushing on the lower assembly. Slide the assembly inside the pipe, positioning the bushing flange to be flush with the top of the pipe.

3. Place the assembled pieces at the end of a protected work surface, and solder each one. Be careful not to displace the bushings. Concentrate the flame on the copper pipe as you heat the joints, and feed the solder from the bottom. Don't let the solder run into the brass tube.

Step C: Form the Head

1. Clean and flux all the pieces of the head. On a heatproof surface, lay out the head sides, top, and bottom pieces, along with four ½" copper 90° elbows and a ½" copper tee to form a rectangle roughly 12 × 14" (30.5 × 35.5 cm) (see diagram on page 13).

2. Cut a 39" (99 cm) piece of ¼" copper tubing and slightly flatten each end. Clamp one end of the tube to a 1-gallon paint can and wrap almost one whole revolution. Remove the tubing and clamp the opposite end to a 1-quart paint can. Wrap the tubing, in the opposite direction, 1¼ rotations, or just until the two loops intersect one another. Unclamp the tubing and place it on a flat, level soldering surface. Refine the shape until both loops lie flat and the small loop wraps inside itself. Form a slight bend on the open end of the large loop.

3. Lay the shaped tubing inside the copper rectangle, and use large, flat washers to shim the tubing into position. Adjust the tubing until it touches the edge of the frame at the open end of the large loop and at the outer edges of both loops. Clean, flux, and solder these points.

D. *Coil 10-gauge copper wire around a quart paint can, and then cut the wire into 5" pieces. Shape each piece into a leaf; file or grind the end of each leaf until it's flat.*

Step D: Add the Leaves

1. Cut a 65" (1.65 m) length of 10-gauge copper wire and mark every 5" (12.7 cm) with a black marker. Using a red marker, place another mark 2½" (6.35 cm) from one end and every 5" from that mark.

2. Clamp and wrap the wire around a 1-quart paint can. Remove the coil and use wire cutters to cut the coil at each black mark, yielding thirteen 5" pieces of curved wire.

3. Lightly crimp each piece of wire at the red mark. Use pliers to fold each wire in half to form a leaf shape. File or grind the end of each leaf to form a flat surface where the leaf can be soldered to the vine.

4. Clean and flux the contact spots, then use large, flat washers to shim the leaves into position around the copper tubing. Solder the leaves to the vine.

Step E: Insert the Stem & Drill the Holes

1. Insert the 5" stem into the tee, and shim the open end of the stem to be even with the other pieces. Solder each joint and let the assembly cool.

2. Place the head on a flat surface. Along the surface of one side of the head, mark nine points, 1" apart. Repeat on the other side of the head, so the marks face the opposite direction. Finally, lay out five marks, one every 2", along the top of the head.

3. Centerpunch and drill one ⅟₁₆" (1.6 mm) hole at each mark. Be sure to drill the holes through only one wall of the pipe.

Step F: Add the Swivel Joint

Dry-fit the upper assembly of the swivel joint to the tee at the bottom of the sprinkler head (be sure the brass tube is extending down). Flux the mating surfaces and solder the joint.

Step G: Build the Stand & Assemble the Sprinkler

1. Center a ½" brass shower ell on top of a 6" galvanized wicket, and mark the holes. Drill holes in the wicket, and then secure the ell to it, using machine screws and nuts. Spray paint these pieces to match the copper color of the sprinkler. Let the paint dry.

2. Solder a ½" threaded copper adapter to the open end of the stand pipe. When the piece is cool, wrap the threads of the adapter with Teflon™ tape. Screw the adapter into the top of the shower ell and a hose connector to the other.

3. Set the hoop into the stand pipe, mating the upper and lower portions of the swivel joint. Attach a garden hose to the hose connector.

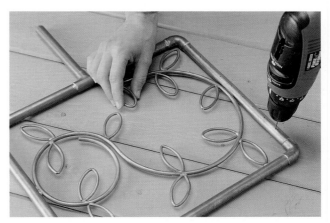

E. *Mark the placement, and then drill holes along the sides and at the top of the head. (Drill through only one wall of each pipe.)*

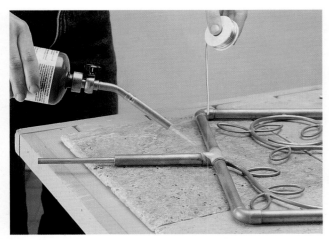

F. *Solder the swivel joint to the tee at the base of the head.*

G. *Assemble the standpipe. Connect a shower ell to one end and a garden hose connector to the other.*

Clay Pot Birdbath

To attract birds to your yard and garden, you need to provide sources of clean water for drinking and for bathing. It may be surprising, but good hygiene is just as important to birds as it is to people. Regular baths discourage parasites and help the birds stay warm—clean feathers actually offer better insulation than dirty ones.

A simple birdbath can be just as effective and attractive as a more elaborate version. This one is merely clay pots and saucers stacked and then secured with a threaded rod and a combination of washers and nuts. Just for fun, we used a texturized paint technique on the clay pots and saucers. Then we added sugar glass beads because—like many people—birds are drawn to a little bit of sparkle.

Place your birdbath in an area that offers resting spots and perches for the birds, but without providing hiding places for predators. An area with trees and bushes nearby is good, for example, as long as there are no low-hanging branches from which a cat could pounce upon the unsuspecting birds.

Birds are creatures of habit. Once they are familiar with a source of food or water, they begin to count on its presence, so keep your birdbath clean and filled throughout the season.

TOOLS & MATERIALS

- Terra-cotta pots: 14" (35.5 cm), 12" (30.5 cm), 9½" (24 cm)
- Terra-cotta saucers: 18" (45.72 cm), 16" (40.64 cm), 12" (30.5 cm)
- Large container of sand
- Drill with ½" (12.7 mm) masonry bit
- Duct tape
- Conical rasp bit
- Water-based masonry paint
- Paint brushes
- Acrylic glaze

- Acrylic paint
- Plastic wrap
- Sparkle dust
- Waterproof sealer/glue/finish, such as Mod Podge Outdoor
- Sugar glass beads
- Rubber washers (5)
- Large flat metal washers (5)
- Threaded rod (48" [1.22 m])
- Nuts (5)
- Silicone caulk
- Acorn nut

HOW TO BUILD A CLAY POT BIRDBATH

Step A: Drill Holes in the Saucers

1. Put duct tape on the bottom of each saucer, then center and mark an X on each saucer, using a ruler and permanent marker. Soak the saucers in water for at least an hour.

2. Fill a large bucket or other container with sand. Set a saucer upside down into the sand so that the edges of the saucer are supported by the sand. At the center mark, drill a hole, using a ½" (12.7 mm) masonry bit. Drill slowly, using light pressure. If necessary, use a conical rasp bit to enlarge the hole. Repeat with each saucer.

A. *Drill a ½" hole at the center of each saucer.*

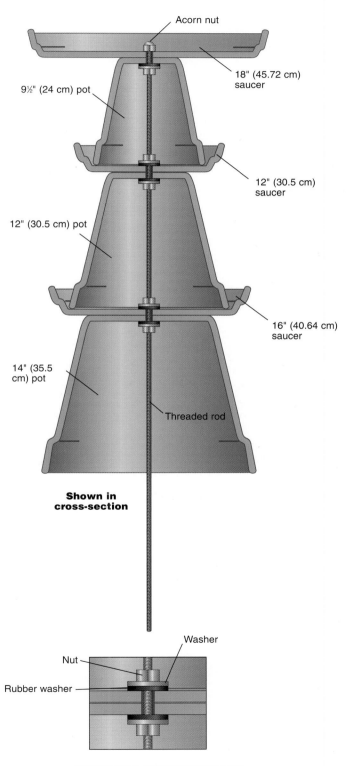

Acorn nut

9½" (24 cm) pot

18" (45.72 cm) saucer

12" (30.5 cm) saucer

12" (30.5 cm) pot

16" (40.64 cm) saucer

14" (35.5 cm) pot

Threaded rod

Shown in cross-section

Washer

Nut

Rubber washer

HARDWARE ASSEMBLY DETAIL
(shown in cross-section)

Step B: Paint the Pots and Saucers for the Base

1. Start with clean, dry terra-cotta pots and saucers. Paint a coat of water-based masonry paint onto the outside of each piece and the interior of the 18″ saucer. After the first coat is dry, apply a second. Let all the pieces dry.

2. Mix a slightly darker or lighter color of acrylic paint and an acrylic glaze, at a ratio of about 10:1. Roughly paint the glaze onto one of the pots. Scrunch up a handful of plastic wrap and use it to pat the wet glaze to produce a crazed texture over the entire pot. Repeat with each pot and saucer, and then let them dry overnight.

3. Seal each piece with a coat of waterproof sealer/glue/finish. Mix a little sparkle dust into the finish when you seal the interior of the 18" saucer.

Step C: Embellish the Saucers

Paint the rim of the 12″ and 16″ saucers with waterproof sealer/glue/finish and then roll them in sugar glass beads.

Step D: Assemble the Base

1. Mark the rod 32½″ (82.5 cm) from one end. Slip a rubber washer and then a flat washer onto the threaded rod and add a nut. Position the washers and nut at the marked location. Slide the 14″ pot onto the rod, facing down. Top it with the 16″ saucer, facing up.

2. Continue alternating pots and saucers, using rubber washers as bumpers, and metal washers and nuts to hold the pots in place.

Step E: Install the Basin

1. Set the base in position in the garden, carefully pressing down to push the rod into the soil. (The buried rod provides stability for the birdbath.)

2. Add the 18" saucer to create the basin. Put a dab of silicone caulk at the edges of the hole to seal any gaps surrounding the threaded rod. Top the threaded rod with an acorn nut.

B. *Paint a base coat on each pot and saucer, and let it dry. Add a glaze and texture it with plastic wrap.*

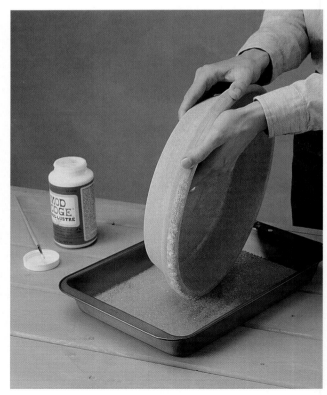

C. *Paint the rims of the 12" and the 16" saucers with Mod Podge Outdoor, and roll them in sugar glass beads.*

TIP: CLEANING A BIRDBATH

Providing a birdbath is the first step; keeping it clean is the second. A well-used birdbath can quickly fill up with debris, such as leaves, feathers, and bits of food. Depending on how much use your birdbath gets, it may need to be cleaned as often as once a week, but certainly every two weeks.

To clean a birdbath, rinse the basin thoroughly, and then scrub its surface with a stiff brush. Next, fill the basin with a 10:1 solution of hot, soapy water and bleach, and let it soak for about 15 minutes.

(Chlorine is toxic to birds, so set the birdbath inside or cover it with a tarp while the solution soaks.) After it has soaked, rinse the bath and scrub it with a brush once again. Finish with a very thorough rinse, and then fill the bath with fresh water.

If you prefer not to use chemicals, use sand to scrub out your birdbath. Just dip a damp cloth into a bag of clean sand, and then scour away the grime. Rinse and refill the bath.

D. *Use a threaded rod, rubber washers, flat washers, and nuts to secure the stack of pots and saucers.*

E. *Top the stack with the 18" saucer, and then use silicone caulk to seal any gaps between the hole and threaded rod. Add an acorn nut to secure the basin.*

Millstone Fountain

In New England, gardeners often use antique well covers for fountains of this type. Around my childhood home in the Ozark Mountains of southern Missouri, people sometimes use antique millstones. Neither type of stone is easy to find these days, and they're quite expensive if you do come across one. But we found that hypertufa (a versatile mixture that includes portland cement and peat moss) provides a practical, inexpensive alternative. If you're looking for a simple, elegant fountain for an existing garden pond, this could be perfect.

Before you begin this project, read the background information on working with hypertufa, found on pages 106 to 107. There you'll find recipes, mixing instructions, and directions for curing hypertufa.

Although you could use either one, we prefer Recipe #2 for projects that will be constantly exposed to water, such as this one.

On this project, timing is critical. Cast the stone at least two months before you plan to put it into a pond. The curing process includes a month of drying time (which is essential) and then another two to three weeks to wash the alkalinity of the portland cement out of the stone. Skipping this final step won't affect the structural integrity of the stone, but the excess alkalinity could alter the water in your pond enough to kill the fish or aquatic plants. Avoid the whole problem by allowing plenty of time for the curing process.

TOOLS & MATERIALS

- Jig saw
- Drill with ⅛" (3 mm) twist bit and 1½" (3.8 cm) spade bit
- Hammer
- Circular saw
- Compass
- Tape measure
- Straightedge
- Aviation snips
- Chisel or paint scraper
- Wire brush
- ⅛" (3 mm) masonite (at least 2 × 4 ft. [61 cm × 1.22 m])
- 2 × 4 (5 × 10 cm) (at least 2 ft. [61 cm])
- 2 × 2 (5 × 5 cm) (at least 2 ft. [61 cm])
- 1" (2.54 cm) wallboard screws
- ¾" (19.05 mm) plywood (4 × 6 ft. [1.22 × 1.82 m])
- 2 × 4 lumber (at least 12" [30.5 cm])
- 2 × 2 lumber (at least 24" [61 cm])
- ¼" (6.35 mm) plywood (scrap at least 12" [30.5 cm] long)
- 1" (2.54 cm) brads
- 2½" (6.35 cm) wallboard screws (4)
- 1½" (3.8 cm)-dia. PVC pipe (6" [15.25 cm])
- Release agent
- Hypertufa recipe #2 (page 106)
- Dust mask
- Rubber gloves
- ¼" (6.35 mm) hardware cloth
- Plastic tarp
- Concrete blocks
- Submersible pump with water delivery tube
- Bricks (2)

A. *Secure two strips of masonite to cleats, using 1" wallboard screws.*

HOW TO BUILD A MILLSTONE FOUNTAIN

Step A: Build the Walls of the Form

1. Cut two 12 × 47½" (30.5 × 121 cm) strips of ⅛" masonite. Along one edge and both ends of each strip, mark and drill an ⅛" hole every 4" (10 cm).

2. Cut a 12" (30.5 cm) cleat from a 2 × 4 and two 12" cleats from a 2 × 2. Butt the ends of the masonite strips together, center them over the 2 × 4 cleat, and fasten them with 1" wallboard screws. Fasten a 2 × 2 cleat flush at each of the other ends, using wallboard screws.

Step B: Build the Base of the Form

1. Cut two 27½"-diameter (70 cm) circles from ¾" plywood, using a jig saw.

2. Stack the circles, carefully align them with one another, then join them, using 1" wallboard screws. Drill a 1½"-diameter (3.8 cm) circle at the center of this base.

3. Make a mark every 14⅜" (36.5 cm) around the circumference of the base. Lay a straightedge so the end touches the mark, and the edge touches a tangent point on the side of the drilled circle. Draw a line along the straightedge. Repeat with each point along the outer circumference of the form. Cut six ¼ × 12" (6.35 mm × 30.5 cm) strips of ¼" plywood; fasten one strip to each line, using 1" brads.

B. *Cut and join two circles of ¾" plywood. Mark placement lines and tack strips of ¼" plywood to the face of the base.*

C. *Attach the masonite wall to the base of the form, and then screw the 2 × 2 cleats together to close the circle.*

D. *Mix the hypertufa and pack a 2" layer onto the floor of the form. Insert a piece of hardware cloth, and add hypertufa until the stone is about 4" thick.*

Step C: Assemble the Form

1. Bend the masonite wall around the base. Starting midway between the cleats, attach the wall to the base, using 1" wallboard screws.

2. To close the ends, screw the cleats together, using 2½" wallboard screws.

3. Set the piece of 1½"-diameter PVC pipe into the hole in the center of the base. Apply release agent to the outside edges of the pipe, the base (including the ¼" strips), and the inside wall of the form.

Step D: Cast the Stone

1. Mix the hypertufa, following the directions on pages 106 to 107. Be sure to wear a dust mask and gloves when handling the dry cement mix and when working with wet cement.

2. Pack hypertufa onto the floor of the form, pressing it down firmly and packing it tightly around the PVC. Continue to add hypertufa until you've created a solid, 2"-thick (5 cm) layer.

3. Using aviation snips, cut a piece of hardware cloth to fit within the form. Settle the hardware cloth into place, then add and pack down the hypertufa until it's approximately 4" (10 cm) thick.

Step E: Allow to Dry & Remove the Forms

1. Cover the form with a plastic tarp, and let the hypertufa dry for at least 48 hours. If the weather is warm, remove the tarp and mist the hypertufa with water occasionally during the curing process.

2. Remove the screws from the form, working carefully so the form can be reused, if desired. If the stone appears to be dry enough to handle without damaging it, remove the PVC pipe in the center. If not, let the hypertufa dry for another 24 hours, then remove the pipe. Turn the stone over and pull away the plywood base.

Step F: Complete the Curing Process

1. If you want the stone to have a weathered look, now is the time to create it. Working slowly and carefully, use a hammer to rough-up the edges of the stone. To add texture, gouge grooves on the surface, using a chisel or paint scraper. Complete the aging process by roughing the entire stone with a wire brush.

2. Cover the stone with plastic, and let it cure for about a month. Uncover it at least once a week, and mist it with water to slow down the curing process. Although it's natural to be impatient, don't rush this step. The more slowly the hypertufa cures, the stronger and more durable the stone will be.

3. Unwrap the stone and let it cure outside,

uncovered, for several weeks. Periodically wash it down with water to remove some of the alkaline residue of the concrete (which would otherwise endanger the plants or fish in your pond). Adding vinegar to the water speeds this process somewhat, but it still takes several weeks. (See page 107 for more details on the curing process.)

Step G: Install the Pump & Stone

1. Place concrete blocks in the pond, positioned to support the stone and bring it slightly above the surface of the water. Between the blocks, set two bricks to support the pump. Center the pump on top of the bricks, then extend the electrical cord up over the bank and out to the nearest GFCI receptacle.

2. Turn on the pump and adjust the flow valve, following manufacturer's instructions. Test and adjust until the bubbling effect or spray appeals to you. Keep in mind that the first 4 to 5" (10 to 13 cm) of spray are covered by the stone.

3. Center the hole in the stone over the water delivery tube of the pump, and lower the stone onto the blocks in the pond.

4. Arrange plants and stones on the bank to disguise the electrical cord as it exits the pond.

E. *When the hypertufa has cured for at least 48 hours, remove the form walls, the PVC pipe, and the plywood base.*

F. *Using a wire brush, chisel, and hammer, remove the stone's sharp edges and create a weathered texture.*

G. *Stack bricks and concrete blocks to support the stone and the pump. Place and adjust the pump, and set the stone on top of the blocks, centered over the pump.*

Accessories

Webster's Dictionary tells us that an accessory is an object or device "not essential in itself but adding to the beauty, convenience, or effectiveness of something else." When it comes to garden accessories I have to respectfully disagree. Beauty—appeal to the eyes, ears, nose, and soul—is the garden's whole reason for being. That which adds beauty is essential.

Accessories have more than aesthetic appeal: They give gardeners something to work on and play with once the basic structure of the garden is in place. We always face seasonal tasks, such as dividing and transplanting, and like Hope, weeding springs eternal; but there are limits to the number of major borders or beds that can be added to one garden. Fortunately, when we're in the mood to create, there's almost always room for accessories. And if your own garden's already well appointed, remember this: Garden accessories make wonderful gifts.

IN THIS CHAPTER:

Wobbler

During the growing season, a wobbler makes a topiary-like support for ivy, sweet pea, or bean vines, and during the winter it warms the garden with candles or miniature lights.

This is another project that makes ingenious use of copper plumbing materials. The construction is so simple that you can easily make several for your own garden—and maybe one or two to give as gifts. The spiral is shaped by forming flexible copper tubing into a coil and then elongating the coil into a tree-like shape. Flexible copper tubing is malleable and fairly forgiving as long as you don't crimp it, so the key is to work slowly, using a firm but gentle touch. The stand is merely a piece of copper pipe set in a paint can filled with quick-setting concrete, and the candle holders are copper end caps supported by reshaped pipe straps.

During the holiday season it should be easy to find miniature candles for the wobbler, but they're available year-round at specialty candle retailers, on the internet, or through catalogs. These small candles burn down quickly, so keep a supply on hand.

If you train plants to twine up your wobbler, be sure to tie the tendrils loosely with soft ties, such as strips cut from old cotton t-shirts. And keep in mind that container-grown plants require more careful watering than plants in open ground.

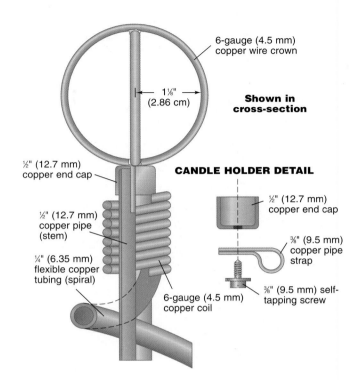

6-gauge (4.5 mm)
copper wire crown

1⅛"
(2.86 cm)

**Shown in
cross-section**

½" (12.7 mm)
copper end cap

½" (12.7 mm)
copper pipe
(stem)

¼" (6.35 mm)
flexible copper
tubing (spiral)

6-gauge (4.5 mm)
copper coil

CANDLE HOLDER DETAIL

½" (12.7 mm)
copper end cap

⅜" (9.5 mm)
copper pipe
strap

⅜" (9.5 mm) self-
tapping screw

TOOLS & MATERIALS

- Tubing cutter
- Circular saw
- Level
- Jig saw
- Drill
- Hammer
- Screwdriver
- Channel-type pliers
- Pop rivet gun
- Locking pliers
- Aviation snips
- Propane torch
- Awl
- Pliers
- Empty 1-gallon (4-l) paint can
- Quick-setting concrete mix
- ½" (12.7 mm) rigid copper pipe (65" [1.65 m])
- Two scraps of plywood, (each at least 20" [50.8 cm] square)

- Duct tape
- 1" (2.54 cm) deck screws (6)
- ¼" (6.35 mm) flexible copper tubing (25 ft. [7.6 m])
- 6-gauge (4.5 mm) copper wire
- 2"-dia. (5-cm) tin can
- ¾" (19.05 mm) copper pipe or wood dowel
- ½" (12.7 mm) copper end caps (21)
- Flux and flux brush
- Solder
- ⅜" (9.5 mm) copper pipe straps (20)
- #3-32 × ⅜" (9.5 mm) self-tapping screws (20)
- ½ × 4" (12.7 mm x 10 cm) candles
- Compass
- Steel pop rivets

HOW TO BUILD A WOBBLER
Step A: Build the Stem Assembly

1. Cut a 65" (1.65 m) length of ½" copper pipe, using a tubing cutter.

2. Mix quick-setting concrete, following manufacturer's instructions. Pour the concrete into a 1-gallon paint can.

3. Set the copper pipe in the center of the paint can. Use a level to make sure the pipe is plumb, then tape it in position, using duct tape. Set this assembly aside for several hours or until the concrete is thoroughly dry.

Step B: Build a Bending Jig & Form the Spiral

1. Cut two 20" (50.8 cm) squares from scrap plywood. Centered on one of the squares, mark a 16"-diameter (40.64 cm) circle, then use a jig saw to cut out the circle.

2. Use 1" deck screws to secure the frame of the cutout to the remaining plywood square, creating a jig that will contain the flexible tubing as you form it into a coil.

3. Cut a 25-ft.(7.6 m) length of ¼" flexible copper tubing. Using channel-type pliers, flatten the first 2 to 3" (5 to 7.6 cm) of one end of the tubing. If necessary, use a hammer to smooth the flattened tubing.

4. Position the opposite (round) end of the tubing

A. *Plant a 65" piece of ½" copper pipe in a paint can filled with quick-setting concrete. Make sure the pipe is plumb, then tape it into position and let the concrete dry.*

at the outer edge of the bending jig. Form the tubing into a loose coil until you reach the flattened end. Leave about 1" (2.54 cm) between the loops in the outer edges, and gradually form the loops closer together as you near the center of the coil.

5. Grasp the flattened end and lift the coil from the bending jig. Pull up on the center of the coil and gently reshape the coil until it forms a tree-shaped spiral approximately 50" (1.27 m) tall.

Step C: Attach the Spiral to the Stem Assembly

1. Position the stem assembly inside the spiral, with the flattened tubing near the top of the stem. Use channel-type pliers to bend the flattened tubing around the stem, continuing the general spiral shape up and around the stem. Stop about ½" from the end of the stem. Clamp the spiral in place with locking pliers.

2. Drill two pilot holes through the tubing and stem, then secure the spiral to the stem, using a pop rivet gun and steel pop rivets.

3. Cut one 7½" (19 cm) and one 6⅝" (16.83 cm) length of 6-gauge copper wire. Shape the 6⅝" length of wire around a 2"-dia. tin can, forming a circle. Shape the 7½" piece of wire around the tin can. At the end of the resulting circle, bend the wire at a 90°

B. *Flatten 2 to 3" of one end of a 25-ft. length of ¼" flexible copper tubing, then push the tubing into a bending jig, forming a loose coil. Reshape the coil into a tree-shaped spiral.*

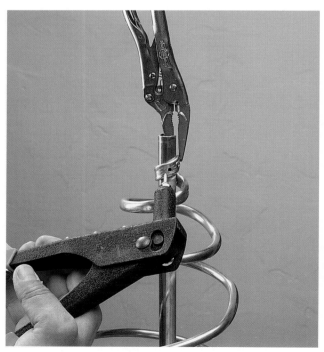

C. *Clamp the spiral into position on the stem assembly, then drill pilot holes and secure the spiral to the stem, using pop rivets.*

D. *To form candle holders, shape ⅜" copper pipe straps around the spiral. Secure one ½" copper end cap to each pipe strap, using ⅜" self-tapping screws.*

angle to form a stem approximately 1" long.

4. To form the crown, place the first circle inside and perpendicular to the second. Gently reshape the wire to form the circles into a crown. At the top of the crown, mark the intersection of the circles, then use aviation snips to cut a V-shaped notch in the wire on the inside face of the outer circle (see diagram on page 27).

5. Balance the circles in the open end of the tin can, with the inner circle resting in the notch on the outer circle. Flux and solder the intersection of the circles (see pages 104 to 105). Let the joint cool.

6. Drill a pilot hole in the center of a ½" copper end cap. Insert the stem of the crown into the pilot hole in the end cap. Flux and solder the intersection of the wires to the end cap and let the joint cool.

7. Wrap 6-gauge wire in eight tight loops around a piece of ¾" copper pipe or wood dowel. Cut the wire, then slip the coil off of the pipe or dowel. Slide the coil down over the stem of the wobbler, then place the crown at the top of the stem.

Step D: Add the Candle Holders

1. Wrap each of the ⅜" pipe straps around the tubing so the flanges meet. Use an awl to center-punch each of the remaining end caps, then secure a reshaped pipe strap to the bottom of each end cap with a ⅜" self-tapping screw.

2. Back the screws out enough to open the straps, then position these assemblies so they form candle holders at the outside edge of the spiral, roughly equidistant from one another. Use pliers to gently flex each candle holder until it's vertical.

3. Carefully screw one ½ × 4" candle onto the screw at the center of each candle holder.

VARIATIONS: WOBBLER WITH MINIATURE LIGHTS OR IVY

The glow of a garden by candlelight is appealing, but not always practical. If you prefer to use miniature lights on your wobbler, follow the same procedure, but omit Step D. Then string miniature lights along the tubing and secure them with fishing line or floral tape.

You may also want to omit the candle holders if you plan to train ivy to grow on your wobbler. Simply select a large pot or other planting container with adequate drainage, add a 2" (5 cm) layer of washed gravel, and position the wobbler in the center. Fill the planting container with potting soil and plant the ivy. As it grows, loosely tie the tendrils along the tubing, and prune as necessary to retain the spiral shape.

Right: Miniature lights bathe the wobbler in sparkling swirls that add a special glow to dinner on the deck, parties in the garden, or holiday lighting schemes.

Far right: Training ivy to grow along a wobbler creates a topiary-like ornament that looks right at home on a deck or patio or beside a sidewalk or entry.

Windmill

One of the great joys of building garden ornaments is creating something of value from very simple materials. This project shows you how to convert a tin can, some pieces of step flashing and a handful of hardware into a unique windmill.

Although it appears to be strictly ornamental, the windmill actually carries out several tasks in a garden. First, it adds motion to the scene, dancing in celebration of one of the fundamental forces of nature—the wind. It indicates wind velocity and direction as it contributes an interesting vertical element to a bed or border. And, finally, the post offers a support for twining plants, such as morning glory, scarlet runner, or honeysuckle.

Some of the items on the materials list may seem a little odd. For instance, we specify a chicken broth can for the windmill hub simply because the broth drains easily. Any 14½ oz. (428 ml) can containing liquid rather than solids will work just fine. The toilet flange is used simply as a form around which to bend wire; any 8"-dia. (20.32 cm) round object will do just as well.

Building the axle that enables the windmill to spin is a somewhat complex process, but it's not difficult. Use the drawings on page 31 to develop a clear image of what you're trying to accomplish, and then go through the process one step at a time. Both this axle and the spindle are built on the same principle as the stem of the copper sprinkler pictured on pages 12 through 15.

TOOLS & MATERIALS

- Razor knife
- Straightedge
- Tape measure
- Drill and ³⁄₃₂", ½" bits
- Awl
- Tubing cutter
- Propane torch
- Bench grinder or rotary tool
- Workbench vise
- Hacksaw
- Aviation snips
- Pliers
- Flat file
- 12-ft. (3.65 m) 4 × 4 (10 × 10 cm)
- ½" (12.7 mm) spade bit
- 14½ oz. (428 ml) can of chicken broth
- Permanent marker
- 6-gauge (4.5 mm) copper wire
- 1½" (3.8 cm) wood dowel
- PVC toilet flange or other 8"-dia. (20.32 cm) form
- Flux and flux brush

- Clamp
- Solder
- ½" (12.7 mm) copper pipe straps (6)
- 5 × 7" (12.7 × 17.8 cm) flat step flashing (6)
- #3–32 × ¼" (6.35 mm) machine screws (12)
- ½" (12.7 mm) copper pipe (5 ft. [1.5 m])
- ⅜" (9.5 mm) (o.d.) brass tube
- ½" (12.7 mm) (o.d.) × ⅜" (9.5 mm) (i.d.) bronze bushings (3)
- ¹¹⁄₃₂" (8.7 mm) round brass tubing
- ⁵⁄₁₆" (8 mm) round brass tubing
- Brass hinge pin bushings (GM #38375) (4)
- 12 × 18" (30.5 × 45.72 cm) piece of 18-gauge (1.25 mm) galvanized sheet metal
- #3-32 × ⅝" (15.86 mm) machine screws and nuts (4)
- 1" (2.54 cm) dowel
- ½" (12.7 mm) copper tee
- Small cotter pin

HOW TO BUILD A WINDMILL

Step A: Construct the Hub

1. Use a razor knife and a straightedge to cut the label off the tin can, keeping the label in one piece. Lay it flat and mark six equal divisions onto the label, then tape it back in place, marked side out.

2. At each end of the can, use a fine-tip permanent marker to transfer the six divisions to the rim. With the marker and a straightedge, draw lines connecting the marks that lie directly opposite one another. The point where the marks intersect is the exact center of the can.

3. Punch the centerpoint, using an awl, then drill a ½" (12.7 mm) hole in one end of the can. Drill slowly—the drill will jump when the bit breaks through the metal. Empty the contents of the can and wash it out, then drill a ½" hole in the other end of the can.

4. On each end of the can, use an awl to punch a hole at each mark, as close to the rim as possible.

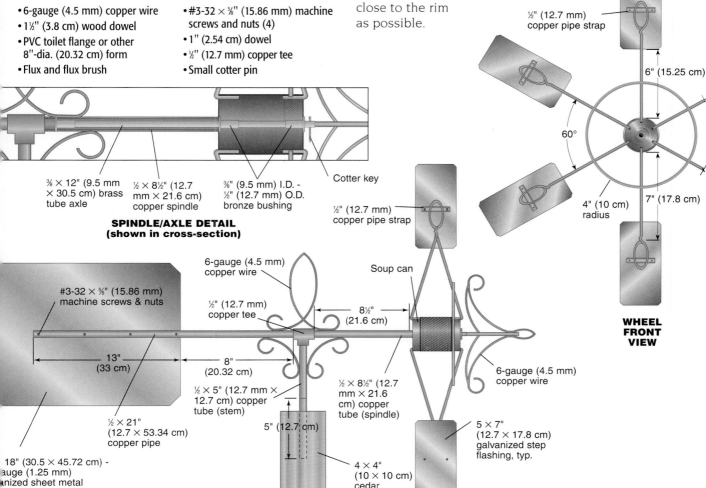

⅜ × 12" (9.5 mm × 30.5 cm) brass tube axle

½ × 8½" (12.7 mm × 21.6 cm) copper spindle

⅜" (9.5 mm) I.D. - ½" (12.7 mm) O.D. bronze bushing

Cotter key

SPINDLE/AXLE DETAIL (shown in cross-section)

½" (12.7 mm) copper pipe strap

½" (12.7 mm) copper pipe strap

6" (15.25 cm)

60°

4" (10 cm) radius

7" (17.8 cm)

WHEEL FRONT VIEW

#3-32 × ⅝" (15.86 mm) machine screws & nuts

6-gauge (4.5 mm) copper wire

½" (12.7 mm) copper tee

Soup can

8½" (21.6 cm)

6-gauge (4.5 mm) copper wire

13" (33 cm)

8" (20.32 cm)

½ × 5" (12.7 mm × 12.7 cm) copper tube (stem)

5" (12.7 cm)

½ × 8½" (12.7 mm × 21.6 cm) copper tube (spindle)

½ × 21" (12.7 × 53.34 cm) copper pipe

18" (30.5 × 45.72 cm) - auge (1.25 mm) nized sheet metal

4 × 4" (10 × 10 cm) cedar

5 × 7" (12.7 × 17.8 cm) galvanized step flashing, typ.

Step B: Form the Spokes

1. Cut seven 24" (61 cm) lengths of 6-gauge bare copper wire. Set one piece of wire aside—it will become the rim later in the process. On each of the remaining six pieces, mark the centerpoint (12" [30.5 cm]), then make a mark 1" (2.54 cm) from

A. *Drill a ½" hole at the intersection of the division marks, and empty the can. Punch a hole at each division mark, as close to the rim as possible. Repeat on the other end of the can.*

each end. Lightly crimp the wires on these end marks and bend the 1" segments back toward each other, slightly more than 90°.

2. Hold a length of wire with the mark centered on a 1½" dowel. Wrap the wire tightly around the dowel and twist it twice. Try to keep the twists even. Remove the wire from the dowel and repeat with five more wires. Make sure all six spokes are identical—adjust if necessary.

3. Adjust the pitch of the spokes by slipping each spoke back onto the dowel and twisting until the plane of the spoke lies at a 45° angle to the dowel.

Step C: Assemble the Hub & Spokes

1. To form the rim, wrap the remaining 24"-length of 6-gauge wire around a PVC toilet flange or other round, 8"-dia. form. Snip the ends of the wire to form a perfect circle. (When the wire is released, don't worry if it springs to a slightly larger diameter.)

2. Insert the bent segments of each spoke into the tin-can hub—one in a hole at the top and one in the corresponding hole at the bottom of the can.

3. Place the assembly on a soft, thick surface, such as a pillow. Position the spokes opposite one another, using the marks on the can as reference points. Place the rim over the spokes, with the open ends of the circle positioned between two sets of spokes. Mark each point where the rim meets a spoke.

4. Move the assembly to a level soldering surface,

B. *To make a spoke, cut a 24" length of 6-gauge copper wire. Bend the ends of the wire back toward one another, slightly more than 90°. Next, wrap the wire around a 1½" dowel and twist it to create two tight, even twists.*

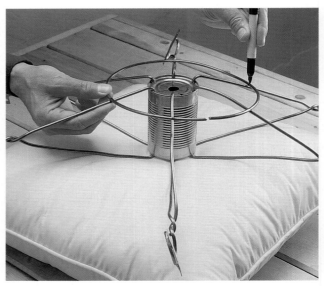

C. *Insert the spokes into the hub, then set the rim in position and mark the points where the spokes meet the rim. Move the assembly to a soldering surface and solder the spokes in place.*

then flux and solder the marked contact points (see pages 104 to 105).

5. Flatten six ½" copper pipe straps. On each spoke, clamp a flattened strap to the face of the loop, positioned so that the strap is centered across the loop, and the holes in the strap overhang evenly. Flux and solder the straps to the wire loops.

Step D: Add the Blades

1. For the blades, trim ½" (12.7 mm) off of each corner of each piece of step flashing, using aviation snips.

2. Position each blade on a spoke with the outer edge of the pipe strap 3" (7.62 cm) from one end of the blade and centered from side to side. Mark reference points through the holes, then remove the blades and drill a ³⁄₃₂" (2.38 mm) hole at each mark.

3. Reposition the blades and fasten each one with a pair of #3-32 × ¼" machine screws.

Step E: Construct the Spindle

1. Cut an 8½" (21.6 cm) length of ½" copper pipe for the spindle and a 12" (30.5 cm) length of ⅜" o.d. brass tube for the axle. Test-fit a ½ × ⅜" bushing inside each end of the ½" copper pipe. If necessary, use a rotary tool or a bench grinder to slightly shape the flange of each bushing so it fits snugly within the pipe. Note: Using a scrap of the ⅜" tubing as a handle helps you get a uniform edge.

2. On the 12" length of ⅜" brass tube, mark a point 4½" (11.43 cm) (the length of the hub plus ½" [12.7 mm]) from one end. Apply flux to the tube at this index mark and at the opposite end. Slide two of the bushings onto the brass tube, both with their raised flanges pointing toward the fluxed end of the tube. Position one bushing with its flange at the index mark and the other flush with the fluxed end of the tube. Solder these bushings in place and allow them to cool.

3. To complete the spindle assembly, slide this axle assembly inside the copper pipe until the flange of the bushing at the index mark is flush with the end of the pipe. Flux this joint and solder it in place.

4. Slide the tin-can hub onto the axle, followed by another bushing with its barrel inside the hub and its flange snug against the end of the hub. Mark this position on the brass tube and remove the hub and bushing. Measure an additional ¹⁄₃₂" (0.8 mm) beyond the mark and drill a ³⁄₃₂" (2.38 mm) hole all the way through the brass tube. Set this spindle assembly aside.

Step F: Make the Stem

Note: For photos of this step, refer to the Copper Sprinkler project, pages 12 through 15.

1. Cut one 5" (12.7 cm) piece and one 6" (15.25 cm) piece of ½" copper pipe, using a tubing cutter. Also cut one 2" (5 cm) and one 4" (10 cm) piece of ¹¹⁄₃₂" brass tubing, and one 6" (15.25 cm) piece of ⁵⁄₁₆" brass tubing. Deburr the pieces, being careful not to flare the ends; use a wire brush or emery cloth to polish the ends.

2. Test-fit the bushings inside the 5" piece of

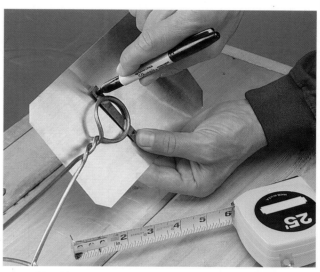

D. *Position blades so that the lower edge of the strap is 3" from the lower edge of the blade. Mark reference points through the strap holes, drill pilot holes, then fasten the blades to the spokes, using machine screws.*

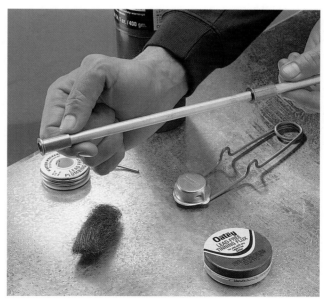

E. *On a 12" length of ⅜" brass tube, position one bushing 4½" from the end of the tube and another at the opposite end, with the flanges facing forward.*

G. *On a 21" length of ½" copper pipe, mark and cut a centerline, 13" long, then slit the pipe along this line. Drill holes in the pipe, then mark and drill corresponding holes in the tail. Secure the tail to the pipe with machine screws.*

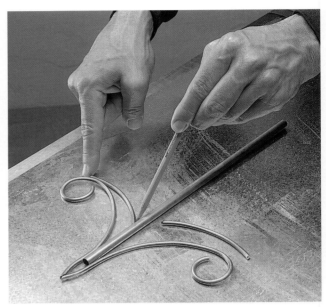

H. *Form arcs of 6-gauge copper wire, then place them around an 8" length of brass tube to form an arrow. Flux the joints and solder the pieces in place.*

copper. If necessary, use a rotary tool or a bench grinder to slightly shape the flanges of the bushings so they fit snugly within the pipe.

3. To form the upper assembly, slide a bushing onto each end of the 2" length of ¹¹⁄₃₂" brass tubing, with the flanges facing the ends of the tube. Set the flange of one bushing back ⅛" (3 mm) from the end of the tube. Position the other bushing flush with the opposite end. Slide the 6" length of ⁵⁄₁₆" brass tubing inside the ¹¹⁄₃₂" tube, positioning the inner tube to protrude ⅜" (9.5 mm) beyond the top (setback) bushing.

4. To form the lower assembly, slide a bushing onto each end of the 4" piece of ¹¹⁄₃₂" brass tubing, flanges facing outward, flush with the ends of the tube.

5. Begin soldering at the top of the upper assembly. Heat all three pieces—the ⁵⁄₁₆" tube, the ¹¹⁄₃₂" tube, and the bushing. These pieces heat up quickly: Be careful not to overheat them. Feed solder into the joint between the two brass tubes first, then feed solder into the bushing joint, approaching that joint from the side opposite the flange.

6. Solder the three remaining bushing joints, each time feeding the solder into the joint from the side opposite the flange.

7. Flux the inside of the 5" piece of ½" pipe and the flange of the bushing on the upper assembly. Slide

the assembly inside the pipe, positioning it so the lower bushing is flush with the end of the pipe.

8. Flux the inside of the 6" piece of copper and the shoulder of one bushing on the lower assembly. Slide the assembly inside the pipe, positioning the bushing flange to be flush with the top of the pipe.

9. Place the assembled pieces at the edge of a protected work surface, and solder each one, being careful not to displace the bushings. Concentrate the flame on the copper pipe as you heat the joints. Feed the solder from the bottom, and don't let the solder run into the brass tube.

Step G: Construct the Tail

1. Cut a 21" (53.34 cm) length of ½" copper pipe. To slit this pipe to accommodate the tail's sail, mark a 13"-long (33-cm) centerline on both sides of the pipe. Clamp the pipe in a workbench vise or comparable pipe vise, then cut down the centerline, using a hacksaw with its blade positioned at 90°. (This cut can be a workout. Try cutting 4" [10 cm] at a time, then letting 4" more out of the vise. Use full strokes of the saw for an accurate, efficient cut.)

2. Turn the pipe 90° in the vise. Starting ½" from the cut end, make four marks—one every 4". Center punch these positions, then drill ³⁄₃₂" holes, perpendicular to the cut line.

3. Trim ¾" (19.05 mm) off the corners of a 12 × 18"

I. *Assemble the spindle, tail, and upper assembly of the stem, and a ½" copper tee, then use a straightedge to make sure they're aligned properly. Flux and solder the pieces in place.*

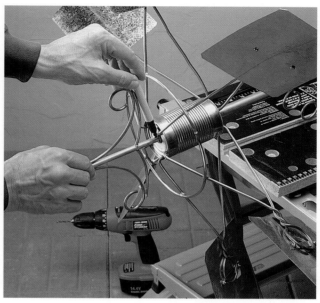

J. *Insert the shaft of the arrow into the axle, with the back of the arrow positioned about 1" from the spokes of the wheel. Mark and drill a hole through the shaft. Pin the shaft in place with a cotter pin.*

piece of galvanized sheet metal and then mark a centerline from end to end. Slide the sheet metal into the slot in the pipe, aligning it so the centerline is visible through the screw holes. Mark the sheet metal through these screw holes, then remove it and drill one ³⁄₃₂" hole at each mark. Assemble the tail, using #3-32 × ⅝" machine screws and nuts.

Step H: Make the Arrow

1. Cut a 27" (68.58 cm) piece of 6-gauge bare copper wire. Mark off positions at 3½" (8.9 cm), 7" (17.8 cm), and 17" (43 cm). Wrap the wire around an 8"-dia. form, such as a PVC toilet flange. Once the ring is formed, cut it at the marks. This process yields two 3½" (8.9 cm) arcs and two 10" (25.4 cm) arcs.

2. At one end of each of the 10" arcs, slightly bend the wire in the opposite direction of the arc to form a slight curve for the point of the arrow. Bend the opposite end of the wire around a 1" dowel to form the decorative accent at the back of the arrow.

3. Cut an 8" (20.32 cm) length of ¹¹⁄₃₂" o.d. brass tubing for the shaft of the arrow. On a level soldering surface, arrange the 10" pieces around the shaft, forming the tip of the arrow, then place one of the 3½" pieces behind each of the 10" pieces to form the arrow shape. Use a flat file to bevel the ends of the wires at the intersections, then flux and solder the joints.

Step I: Connect the Spindle, Tail & Stem

1. Flux the spindle, tail, and upper assembly of the stem and join them (see diagram, page 31) with a ½" copper tee. Lay out the assembly on a level soldering surface and use a straightedge along the top to check for alignment. Adjust if necessary, then solder each joint and let the assembly cool.

2. On one end of a 12 ft. (3.65 m) 4 × 4 (10 × 10 cm), mark the diagonals to find the center. Use a ½" spade bit to bore a 5¾" (14.6 cm) hole straight down the center of the 4 × 4. Gently tap the lower assembly of the stem into this hole.

Step J: Assemble the Windmill

1. Slide the hub and its bushing onto the spindle, then slide the shaft of the arrow into the axle of the hub. Position the back of the arrow approximately 1" from the spokes of the wheel. Mark the shaft of the arrow through the hole in the axle, then remove the shaft and drill a ³⁄₃₂" hole all the way through the tubing at that mark. Slide the shaft of the arrow back into the axle and align all four holes. Pin the shaft in place with a cotter pin.

2. Dig a hole 30" (76 cm) deep, mix cement, and set the post in the desired location.

3. Insert the upper assembly of the stem into the lower assembly (lodged in the 4 × 4).

Wire Rabbit Bean Cage

No matter how much we resent the damage rabbits sometimes do, few of us can resist the image of one bounding through our garden. This wire rabbit is more appealing than the live version in one way: It has no interest whatsoever in nibbling at your lilies or your lettuces.

Tim contrived this clever way to attach the rabbit to a widely available type of bean cage, which looks great covered by pole beans, morning glories, or sweet peas. Another option is to create a sturdy plant stake to support the rabbit, using a length of ½" copper pipe joined to an upper stem of ¼" flexible copper tubing with a ¼ × ½" reducing coupling. Or, you could make the stem itself 24 to 36" long and

stick it directly into a large pot of ornamental grass —your rabbit will appear to be leaping over a field or meadow.

You can find 8-gauge bare copper wire in the electrical department of most hardware stores and home centers. It's typically sold by the foot, measured out from large spools. If you straighten and then coil the wire before you begin to shape it, you'll find it more malleable.

You can buy bell wire in the electrical department, too. It, however, comes with a plastic covering that needs to be stripped away. You can use a utility knife to strip wire, but it's much easier and safer to use an inexpensive tool known as a wire stripper.

TOOLS & MATERIALS

- Pliers
- Wire stripper
- Drill and ⁵⁄₁₆" (8 mm) twist bit
- Propane torch
- Permanent marker
- 8-gauge (4 mm) copper wire
- Masking tape
- Bell wire
- Solder
- Flux and flux brush

- Wire cutter
- Copper pot scrubber
- ¼" (6.35 mm) flexible copper tubing (2 ft. [61 cm])
- ⅜" (9.5 mm) flexible copper tubing (1 ft. [30.5 cm])
- ⁵⁄₁₆" (8 mm) threaded rod (6" [15.25 cm])
- ⁵⁄₁₆" (8 mm) nuts (2)
- Wire bean cage
- Rubber mallet

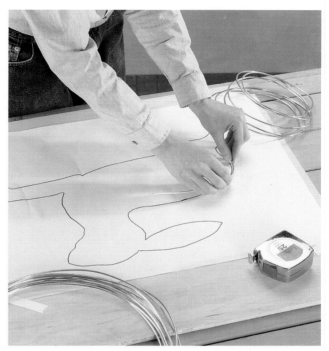

HOW TO BUILD A WIRE RABBIT BEAN CAGE

Step A: Prepare Pattern & Wire

1. Using the grid system or a photocopier, enlarge the pattern shown below. (Our rabbit is 24" [61 cm] from the tip of the hind leg to the tip of the front leg.) Tape the pattern to a smooth, flat work surface.

2. Measure the perimeter of the pattern to determine the necessary lengths of wire. (We needed 82" [208.28 cm] for the rabbit's profiles and 32" [81.28 cm] for the center loop.)

A. *Measure the perimeter of the pattern and cut wire to length.*

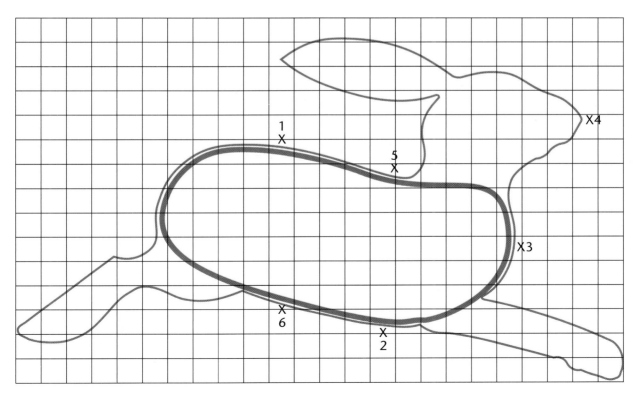

1 square=1" (2.54 cm)

3. Cut 8-gauge wire to length. Partially coil the wire to make it easier to shape.

Step B: Form the Pieces

1. Starting at the mid-back (#1 on the pattern), shape the wire along the contours of the rabbit pattern, using a pair of pliers to create the sharp bends. At the intersection, overlap the ends of the wire, leaving the ends loose.

2. Starting at the mid-bottom (#2), form a second rabbit shape, as described above.

3. Make a center loop for the body of the rabbit, starting at the mid-front (#3).

Step C: Refine the Shapes & Mark the Joints

1. Lay the first rabbit shape on the work surface. Add the center loop and the second rabbit shape. Adjust the pieces until the shapes are as similar as possible. Tape the pieces together at several locations, using masking tape.

2. At each intersection, trim the overlapping wire, and use a permanent marker to indicate the remaining joints as indicated on the pattern.

Step D: Solder the Joints

1. Cut and strip eight 18" (45.72 cm) lengths of bell wire.

2. At the first joint (#4 on the pattern), flux the 8-gauge wire, then wrap a piece of bell wire tightly around all three pieces to join them. Flux and solder the joint. Repeat with the remaining joints (#5 and #6).

3. Flux and solder the wire intersection of each shape. Let the joints cool completely.

Step E: Embellish the Rabbit

1. Bend the legs and ears away from the center loop to add dimension to the rabbit.

2. Thread a piece of bell wire through a copper pot scrubber, and then put the scrubber in place along the center loop, positioning it for the tail. Wrap the wire around the center loop to secure the tail, and then flux and solder the wire as described in Step D.

Step F: Build the Mounting Frame

1. Cut two 20" (50.8 cm) pieces of ¼" flexible copper tubing. Using a rubber mallet, flatten the first ½" (12.7 mm) of each end of each piece of tubing. At the center of each flattened end, drill a ⁵⁄₁₆" (8 mm) hole.

2. Bend each flattened end out, and then shape the tubing into identical, gentle arcs. Lay out the arcs in an X, and mark the centers of the intersec-

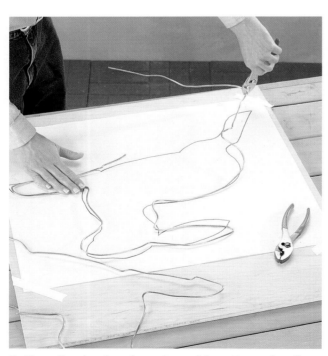

B. *Shape the wire along the contours of the pattern, using pliers to bend sharp angles or curves. Make two rabbit shapes and one center loop.*

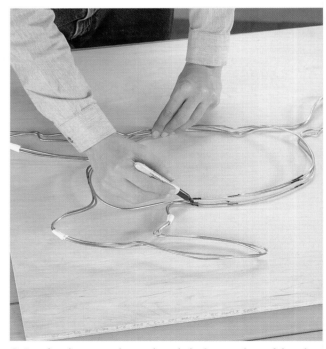

C. *Lay the pieces together and mark the intersections of the wire as well as the joining spots.*

tion. Drill a ⁵⁄₁₆" hole at each mark.

3. Put a nut approximately 1" (2.54 cm) from the end of a 6" length of threaded rod. Stack the tubing in an X and slide that end of the threaded rod through the center holes. Add a nut on the bottom and tighten it until the tubing is held securely together.

4. Cut a 9" (22.86 cm) length of ⅜" flexible copper tubing for the stem. About 2" (5 cm) from one end, bend the tubing at about a 120° angle. Flux the bent portion of the stem. Join the stem to the rabbit shape by wrapping the joint with about 8" (20.32 cm) of bell wire. Flux the wire and then solder the stem to the rabbit shape.

5. Attach the mounting frame to the top of the bean cage, inserting the wire ends into the holes in the mounting frame. Set the rabbit's stem onto the threaded rod. Adjust the angle of the stem until the rabbit appears to be leaping over the bean cage.

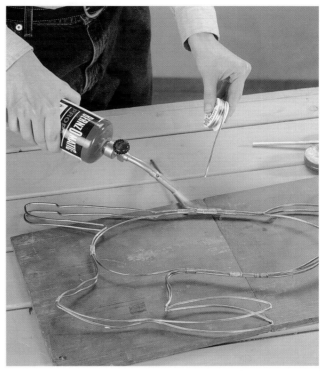

D. *Flux the joints and wrap them with bell wire. Flux the bell wire and then solder the joints.*

E. *Pull the layers away from one another at the ears and legs, giving the rabbit dimension. For the tail, use a piece of bell wire to attach a copper pot scrubber to the center loop.*

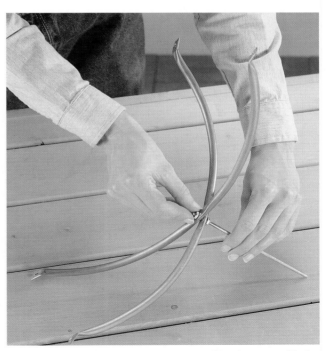

F. *Shape two pieces of ¼" flexible copper tubing into a modified X and drill holes through the center. Use two nuts to secure a threaded rod to this frame.*

Turtle Ornament

In a fascinating novel, *Sparrow*, by Mary Doria Russell, a Texas-born, jet-pilot-trained Jesuit priest declares that if you see a turtle on a fence-post, you can be pretty sure it didn't get there by itself. He then implies that such impossible circumstances must be a sign, evidence of a divine plan.

Since reading *Sparrow*, I've acquired a number of turtles throughout my garden, and this is one of my favorites. Its whimsical presence reminds me to look for and believe in the extraordinary. As gardeners, no matter what else we believe in, we must believe in the extraordinary. After all, we plant bare sticks in the ground and wait for roses.

This turtle, with its distinctive personality, is remarkably easy to create. It's an ingenious combination of simple materials—plywood, chicken wire, expandable foam insulation, and moss.

You'll find spray cans of expandable foam insulation in hardware stores or home centers, in the area where weatherstripping materials are sold. As the name implies, the foam expands as it dries, filling in the chicken wire and providing a base to which the moss can be attached.

We've heard this type of moss variously referred to as puff moss, clump moss, and mood moss. We found it at a floral supplier, labeled as mood moss. No matter what it's called, you'll recognize it when you see it—the individual pieces look just right to be the segments of a turtle's shell.

TOOLS & MATERIALS

- Jig saw
- Drill
- Aviation snips
- ½" (12.7 mm) exterior plywood
- 1 × 3 (2.54 × 7.62 cm) (24" [61 cm])
- Paint brushes
- Exterior latex primer
- Exterior latex paint
- ¾" (19.05 mm) deck screws
- 1¼" (3.8 cm) deck screws
- Exterior wood glue
- Threaded galvanized base flanges (2)
- Stapler and wire staples
- Chicken wire
- Expandable foam insulation
- Clump (or "mood") moss
- Floral staples
- 1½" (3.8 cm) galvanized pipe, threaded at both ends (48" [1.22 m])
- Plastic or galvanized bucket, 1 to 2 gallon (4 to 8 l)
- Quick-setting cement
- Belt sander
- Shovel
- Hand tamp
- Mixing bucket

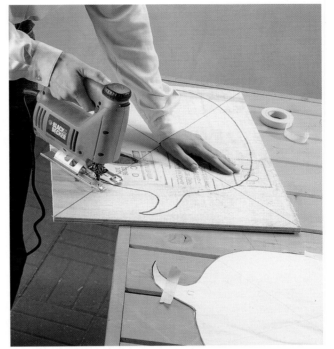

A. *Enlarge the patterns and transfer them onto ½" exterior plywood. Use a jig saw to cut out each piece, and then transfer the markings.*

HOW TO BUILD A TURTLE ORNAMENT

Step A: Cut Out the Pieces

1. Using the grid system or a photocopier, enlarge the patterns below, and then transfer them onto ½" exterior plywood.

2. Cut out the pieces, using a jig saw. Mark the turtle base as indicated on the pattern.

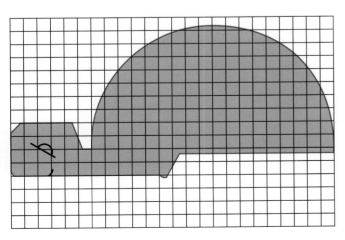

1 square = 1" (2.54 cm)

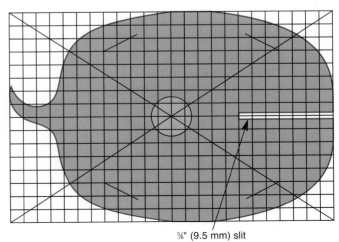

⅜" (9.5 mm) slit

Step B: Complete the Turtle Base

1. Place a base flange at the center of the turtle base and mark its holes onto the plywood. Drill pilot holes and attach the base flange to the turtle base, using ¾" deck screws.

2. Cut four 4½" (11.43 cm) pieces of 1 × 3. On one end of each piece, cut a 25° angle. Round the opposite ends, using a belt sander. Position these legs as indicated on the pattern, and attach each with a pair of angled ¾" deck screws.

3. Apply a coat of exterior latex primer to the turtle base and legs.

Step C: Join the Base & Body

1. Apply exterior wood glue to the sides of the notch in the turtle base and to the lower edge of the shell portion of the turtle body.

2. Slide the turtle body into the notch of the base. At the opposite side, near the tail, drive two 1¼" deck screws through the base and into the body.

Step D: Add the Chicken Wire

Use aviation snips to cut a piece of chicken wire, approximately 30 × 32" (76 × 81.28 cm). Fold under the edges of the chicken wire and staple it to the turtle base.

Step E: Paint the Turtle's Face, Legs, & Tail

1. Using a stenciling brush and several shades of green, paint the turtle's head, legs, and tail with exterior latex paint.

2. Using a fine brush, add the eye and mouth details as indicated on the pattern on page 41.

Step F: Add the Moss

1. Coat the chicken wire with expandable foam insulation. (The insulation will seep through the openings and form a thick layer of foam inside the chicken wire.) Let the foam dry until it's hard (about 24 hours).

2. Use floral staples to attach moss to the foam, trimming clumps as necessary to tailor them to the shell shape.

Step G: Install the Stake

1. Thread a base flange onto a 48" length of 1½" (3.8 cm) threaded, galvanized pipe. Set the base flange in a small bucket, and fill the bucket with quick-setting cement. Let the cement dry.

2. Dig a hole, set the bucket into it, and then replace and tamp the soil as necessary to stabilize the base.

3. Thread the base flange of the turtle onto the top of the galvanized pipe.

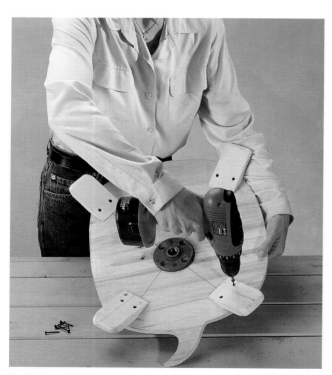

B. *Mark and drill pilot holes, and then attach a base flange to the center of the turtle base. Next, angle pairs of screws to attach the legs to the base.*

C. *Attach the turtle body to the turtle base, using exterior wood glue and screws.*

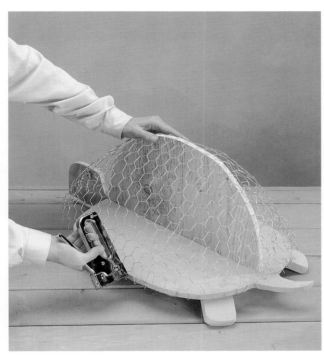

D. *Staple the chicken wire to the turtle base.*

E. *Paint the turtle's head, tail, and legs with exterior latex paint. Add the eye and mouth details.*

F. *Coat the chicken wire with expandable foam insulation. Secure clumps of moss to the hardened foam, using floral staples.*

G. *Set the stand in a bucket of quick-setting cement. When the cement is dry, set the bucket into a hole, and then replace and tamp the soil.*

Placemat Birdfeeder

Attract birds with flights of fancy, as well as their favorite treats. With a sense of style and a touch of humor, this whimsical birdfeeder charms human visitors even as it welcomes avian guests. It also reminds us that all creatures have a place at Nature's table.

Once again, we've used plumbing materials in somewhat surprising ways. The birdfeeder's stand is a simple combination of galvanized pipe and base flanges, which are available in the plumbing department of most hardware stores and virtually all home centers. You should be able to find 48" (1.22 m) lengths of pipe that are pre-cut and pre-threaded. If not, most stores will cut pipe to length and thread the ends for you, free of charge.

When we've used expanded metal grate in the past, we've purchased it at a steel yard and used a reciprocating saw to cut it to size. However, the idea for this birdfeeder really got off the ground when we discovered that precut 12 × 24" (30.5 × 61 cm) pieces are widely available at hardware stores and home centers. Typically used for vents and grilles, they can be found in the area where sheet metal and flashing is displayed. Note: Even on precut pieces, the edges of metal grate can be sharp. Wear heavy gloves when handling it.

Remember that birds are creatures of habit and will quickly come to rely on your feeder as a food source. Keep it well stocked throughout the season, and they will return year after year.

TOOLS & MATERIALS

- Drill
- Reciprocating saw or jig saw with metal-cutting blade
- Grinder or rotary tool
- Shovel
- Pewter or aluminum plate & cup
- 1¼" (3.2 cm) galvanized pipe (48" [1.22 m], threaded at each end)
- Base flanges (2)
- Quick-setting cement
- Caulk gun
- Galvanized bucket or empty paint can
- Soil tamper
- Screwdriver

- ¾" (19.05 mm) expanded metal mesh (12 × 24" [30.5 × 61 cm])
- Panhead machine screws and nuts (2 sets)
- Flat washers (2)
- Locking pliers
- Silicone caulk or Liquid Steel
- Stainless steel knife, fork and spoon
- Pewter or aluminum napkin ring
- Decorative wire mesh
- Heavy gloves
- Mixing bucket
- Permanent marker
- Sand

HOW TO BUILD A PLACEMAT BIRDFEEDER
Step A: Assemble the Base

1. Thread a base flange onto the bottom of a 48" piece of 1¼" galvanized pipe.

2. Mix a small batch of quick-setting cement. Set the pipe into a galvanized bucket or empty paint can, and fill the container with quick-setting cement. Let the cement dry according to manufacturer's directions.

A. *Thread a base flange onto a 48" galvanized pipe, and set that assembly into a bucket or can. Fill the container with quick-setting cement and let it dry.*

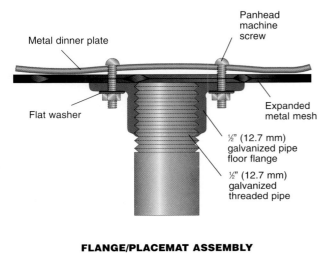

Shown in cross-section

Metal dinner plate

Panhead machine screw

Flat washer

Expanded metal mesh

½" (12.7 mm) galvanized pipe floor flange

½" (12.7 mm) galvanized threaded pipe

FLANGE/PLACEMAT ASSEMBLY

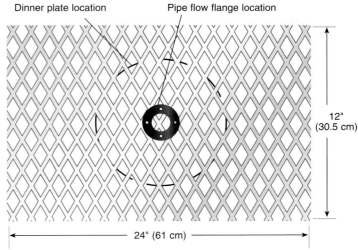

Dinner plate location

Pipe flow flange location

12" (30.5 cm)

24" (61 cm)

Step B: Prepare the Plate

Center a base flange on the back of the plate you've selected; mark two of the holes onto the back of the plate. Carefully drill a ⅜" (9.5 mm) hole at each mark. Drill two or three additional holes (beyond the area of the base flange) for drainage.

Step C: Attach the Placemat & Plate

1. If necessary, cut the expanded metal mesh to size, using a reciprocating saw or a jig saw with a metal-cutting blade. Use a grinder or a rotary tool with an abrasive disk to soften the edges of the mesh.

2. Center the plate on top of the mesh. Through each hole in the plate, thread a panhead machine screw through the mesh and the holes in the base flange; add flat washers and nuts and tighten carefully.

Step D: Add the Details

1. Using silicone caulk or Liquid Steel, secure the silverware and napkin ring to the mesh.

2. Fold a piece of decorative wire mesh into a napkin-like shape. Insert the mesh into the napkin ring, and secure it with a dab of silicone caulk.

3. Drill several drainage holes in the bottom of the cup. Position the cup as for a place setting, and secure it with silicone caulk.

Step E: Install the Feeder

1. Dig a hole 2 to 3" (5 to 7.62 cm) wider and 4" (10 cm) deeper than the bucket of the stand. Keep the edges of the hole fairly straight and the bottom as level as possible. Add about 1" (2.54 cm) of sand to the hole.

2. Set the stand into position, and then thread the feeder assembly onto it. Add or remove sand until the feeder is level.

3. Fill in the hole; tamp the dirt to hold the feeder level and keep it stable.

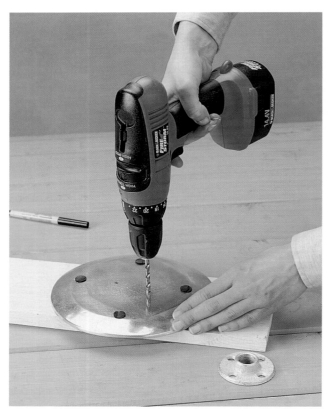

B. *Mark two of the holes of a base flange onto the back of the plate. Drill a hole at each mark.*

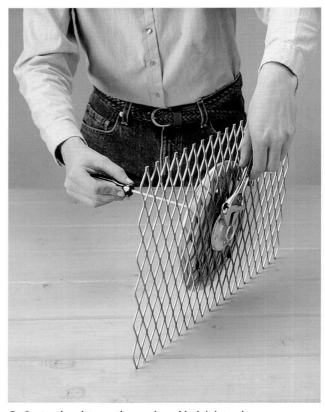

C. *Center the plate on the mesh and bolt it into place.*

TIP: FEEDING BIRDS

Wherever you live, this unique feeder is sure to attract lots of seed-loving birds. And no matter where you place it on your property, the birds will soon find it.

Your feeder will be easier and safer for the birds to use if you place it near sheltering trees, such as alder, birch, maple, or poplar. Shrubs with thick foliage, such as barberry, evergreens, and shrub roses, are also good places for birds to nest. Providing some natural seed plants, such as purple coneflower or black-eyed Susan, in a planting bed will help attract birds to the area as well. Include a source of water nearby, and the birds are sure to return again and again.

A good birdseed mixture may contain sunflower seed, safflower seed, cracked corn, and millet. It will attract sparrows, chickadees, finches, buntings, and many others. Some finches and siskins also like thistle (niger) seed.

Cardinals, jays, and grosbeaks especially like sunflower seeds. These are big birds with big appetites, so always keep a supply of food on hand.

Eastern bluebirds may be attracted by peanut butter mixes and raisins. Baltimore orioles may even visit a feeder if orange halves are available.

And don't forget winged visitors such as mourning doves and juncos. Even though they won't usually come to the feeder tray, they happily eat seeds dropped to the ground by other birds.

D. *Glue the cup, silverware, napkin ring, and decorative mesh into place.*

E. *Dig a hole, add a layer of sand, and adjust until the bucket is level. Refill the hole and tamp the soil to keep the bucket stable.*

Flower Bed

Several years ago, the Minnesota Landscape Arboretum featured an antique iron bed used as a raised-bed planter. Between the cleverness of the idea and the beauty of the old bed, it was simply delightful. I wanted to put one in my own garden, but soon found that antique beds are rather expensive and require a fair amount of space.

The idea just drifted until Tim designed a copper bed for our book, *Garden Style*. When we were working with the prototype, we realized that a miniature version would make a wonderful garden accent. With a wood frame for a planter, it really is perfect—

inexpensive, just the right size, easy to build, and clever as can be.

The best plants for this flower bed are spreading types that will mimic the way a bedspread or coverlet drapes over the edge of a bed. Here we show firefly impatiens, but you could try sweet alyssum, lobelia, or even nasturtium.

If you want to carry the idea to its fullest, add a 10 × 24" (25.4 × 61 cm) layer of dirt to the head end of the 2 × 4 bed frame. The extra height in that area will create the impression of pillows on the bed.

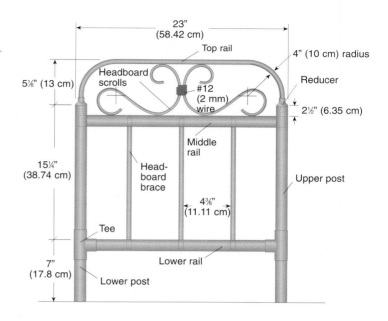

TOOLS & MATERIALS

- Circular saw
- Tubing cutter
- Drill
- Propane torch
- Locking pliers
- Hammer
- Shovel
- Center punch
- 1¼" (3.2 cm) rigid copper (8 ft. [2.44 m])
- ½" (12.7 mm) rigid copper (8 ft. [2.44 m])
- ¾" (19.05 mm) rigid copper (4 ft. [1.22 m])
- ½" (12.7 mm) flexible copper (3 ft. [91.44 cm])
- ¼" (6.35 mm) flexible copper (5 ft. [1.5 m])

- 1¼" (3.2 cm) tees (4)
- 1¼ × ½" (3.2 cm × 12.7 mm) reducers (4)
- Wire brush
- Rotary tool (optional)
- Flux and flux brush
- Solder
- 12-gauge (2 mm) copper wire
- 1-gallon (4-l) paint can
- Scrap of 1½" (3.8 cm) PVC pipe
- 2 × 4 (5 × 10 cm) rough-cut cedar (two 2-ft. [61 cm] boards)
- 10d (7.6 cm) nails
- Rebar (2 ft. [61 cm])
- Copper strapping tape
- Potting soil
- Trailing plants
- 1" (2.54 cm) deck screws (4)

CUTTING LIST

Rigid copper:	Pipe	No.	Size
Headboard upper post	1¼" (3.2 cm) pipe	2	15¼" (38.74 cm)
Footboard upper post			
Lower post		4	5½" (13.97 cm)
Lower rails		2	20¼" (51.44 cm)
Middle rails	¾" (19.05 mm) pipe	2	22⅜" (56.8 cm)
Headboard braces	½" (12.7 mm) pipe	3	14¾" (37.46 cm)
Footboard braces		3	10¾" (27.31 cm)
Flexible copper:			
Top rail	½" (12.7 mm) tubing	2	30" (76.2 cm)
Headboard scrolls	¼" (6.35 mm) tubing	2	30" (76.2 cm)

HOW TO BUILD A FLOWER BED
Step A: Prepare the Posts & Rails

1. Following the cutting list and diagrams, cut all the rigid copper pieces for the headboard and footboard. Mark the holes on the middle and lower rails; center-punch and drill ½" (12.7 mm) holes through only the first wall of each rail.

2. On each upper post, mark the holes for the middle rail. Next, center-punch the hole locations and then drill a ¾" (19.05 mm) hole through only the first wall of each upper post.

Step B: Construct the Frames

1. For the headboard, lay out the middle and lower rails, and fit the braces between them. If

A. *Cut the copper pipe for the headboard and footboard. Mark and drill holes on the upper posts and the middle and lower rails.*

B. *Connect the braces to the middle and lower rails, then add the posts.*

C. *Form the top rail from ½" flexible copper. Make sure that the arcs are equal on each side.*

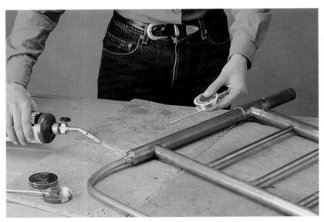

D. *Clean the pipe and fittings and then dry-fit the assemblies. Solder the joints of each, working from the bottom.*

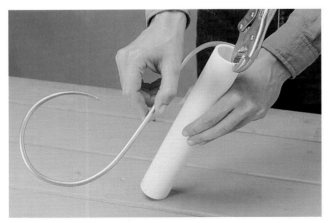

E. *Cut two 30" pieces of ¼" copper tubing. Shape each piece into an S-shaped scroll.*

necessary, use a rotary tool to tailor the holes until the pieces fit securely. Make sure the braces extend as far as possible into the rails.

2. Construct each post, using a 1¼" tee to connect the upper and lower post pieces. Connect the rail and brace assemblies to the posts. Insert the middle rail into the hole on each post and the lower rail into the tee on each side. Make sure the middle rail extends as far as possible into the posts.

3. Top each post with a 1¼ × ½" reducer.

Step C: Add the Upper Rails

Cut a 30" (76 cm) piece of ½" flexible copper for the upper rail of the headboard. On each in turn, form a 4"-radius (10-cm) arc at one end; insert the end of the arc into the reducer at the top of one of the headboard posts. At the other end, shape an arc that brings the end of the rail down to meet the reducer fitting on top of the second post. Trim the ends so the legs of the arcs are of equal length and the rail sits level across the headboard.

Step D: Solder the Assemblies

1. Clean and flux the joints, then dry-fit the pieces of the headboard and then the footboard on a flat, flame-resistant surface. Solder the joints of each, working from the bottom and alternating from side to side. Check from time to time to make sure each assembly remains square and flat. (For more information on soldering, see pages 104 to 105.)

2. Repeat Steps B through D to build the footboard.

Step E: Form the Scrollwork for the Headboard

1. Cut two 30" pieces of ¼" copper tubing. Flatten both ends of each piece of tubing.

2. Use locking pliers to clamp one end of one piece of tubing to the top edge of a 1-gallon paint can. Wrap the tubing about three-quarters of the way around the paint can, then remove it and reclamp the end to a piece of 1½" PVC pipe. Rotate the pipe to curl about 4" of the tubing toward the center of the larger curve.

3. Clamp the opposite end of the tubing to the PVC pipe. Rotate the pipe away from the curve formed in #2, curling about 4" of the tubing around the pipe in the opposite direction, creating an S-shaped scroll.

4. Repeat with the second piece of tubing, checking after each step to make sure it matches the first.

Step F: Add the Scroll to the Headboard

1. Mark the centerpoint of the upper and middle rails on the headboard, and set the first scroll between them. Adjust the tubing into a graceful curve that allows the large curve of the scroll to align with the centerpoint of the headboard and the smaller curve to contact the middle rail about 2½" (6.35 cm) away from the post. Repeat this process to position the opposite scroll.

2. Clean and flux the contact spots on the scrolls and on the upper and middle rails. Solder the scrolls into position. When the center joint cools, wrap it with 12-gauge wire.

Step G: Construct the Planter Frame

1. From rough-cut cedar 2 × 4s, cut four 24" (61 cm) pieces and four 36" (91.44 cm) pieces. At each end of each piece, cut a 1½" (3.8 cm) notch; stagger the position of the notches so that each board is notched at the top on one end and at the bottom on the other.

2. Lay out four boards in a rectangle, interlocking the notches. Drive a 10d nail down into each joint, angling the nail slightly. Add the second course, offsetting the orientation of the notches to produce an alternating pattern.

3. At 18" (45.72 cm) from one end of the planter frame, drill a ⅜" (9.5 mm) hole completely through the bottom course and half-way through the top one. Repeat on opposite side of frame.

Step H: Install the Flower Bed

1. Dig a flat, 2"-deep, 6"-wide (5 × 15.25 cm) trench around the perimeter of a 24 × 36" (61 × 91.44 cm) area. Double dig and, if necessary, amend the soil.

2. On each side of the trench, 18" (45.72 cm) from one end, drive a 12" (30.5 cm) piece of rebar about 7" (17.8 cm) into the ground. Insert the rebar into the holes in the planter frame and settle the frame into position.

3. Cut and shape copper tape into straps for the 1¼" pipe. Position the straps, drill pilot holes, and screw the straps into place with deck screws to attach the headboard and then the footboard to the planter frame.

4. Fill the frame with potting soil and add plants.

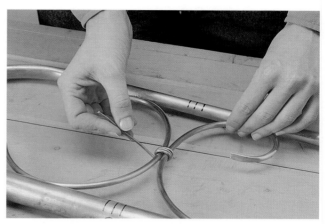

F. *Position the scrolls, flux the pipe at the points of contact, and solder the scrolls into place. Use wire to conceal the joint between the two scrolls.*

G. *Cut, notch, and interlock cedar 2 × 4s to form a frame for the planter. Nail each joint, angling the nails slightly. Make two courses, and offset the orientation of the notches.*

H. *Attach the headboard and footboard to the planter with copper tape and 1" deck screws.*

Copper Chandelier

Imagine this: Dinner on the patio, fragrance waltzing on the evening breeze, candles flickering from a gleaming chandelier. Sounds like something out of a magazine article, right? Not necessarily. In just a few hours, you can make this beautiful chandelier out of a roll of copper tubing, a handful of plumbing standoffs, and a little bit of copper wire. Then all you need is a warm evening and a patio.

The best thing about this project is that it's absolutely doable. Tim really is a genius at designing simple mechanisms and at developing easy ways to shape them from copper. Now that he's done the hard part, all you have to do is read and follow directions carefully. Almost before you know it, you could be dining by candlelight and soaking up compliments.

A copper chandelier makes a wonderful gift for almost any occasion—birthday, anniversary, wedding, Mother's or Father's Day, Christmas. I think anyone with a patio, deck, or garden would be delighted to receive such a unique, handcrafted gift. There's no reason to limit its use to the outdoors, either. Mine hangs in a reading nook in my bedroom.

As you'll see in the diagram on page 53, we used screws to attach the candle cups. Those screws serve a second purpose as well: They help candles stand securely in the cups. You can thread larger or soft candles, such as beeswax, directly onto the screws, but it's much easier to insert the type of small candles shown here if you drill ⅛" (3 mm) pilot holes in them first.

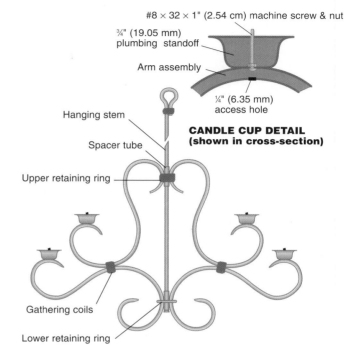

#8 × 32 × 1" (2.54 cm) machine screw & nut

¾" (19.05 mm) plumbing standoff

Arm assembly

Hanging stem

Spacer tube

Upper retaining ring

¼" (6.35 mm) access hole

CANDLE CUP DETAIL (shown in cross-section)

Gathering coils

Lower retaining ring

TOOLS & MATERIALS

- Tubing cutter
- Rubber mallet
- Locking pliers
- Drill
- Wire nippers
- Channel-type pliers
- Band saw or hacksaw
- Propane torch
- ⅜" (9.5 mm) flexible copper tubing (21 ft. [6.4 m])
- 2"-dia. (5 cm) PVC pipe (18" [45.72 cm])
- Foamboard
- Center punch
- Utility tool

- Flaring tool
- 12-gauge (2 mm) copper wire (8 ft. [2.44 m])
- ¾" (19.05 mm) plumbing standoffs (10)
- 8 × 32 roundhead machine screws & nuts (10)
- 1"-dia. (2.54 cm) PVC pipe (18" [45.72 cm])
- ¼" (6.35 mm) flexible copper tubing (3 ft. [91.44 cm])
- Flux and flux brush
- Solder
- Compass
- Protractor
- Masking tape

HOW TO BUILD A COPPER CHANDELIER
Step A: Form the Arms

1. Cut ten 24" (61 cm) lengths of ⅜" flexible copper tubing. Flatten the first 2" (5 cm) of one end of a piece of tubing, using a rubber mallet. Flatten the end completely, then gradually taper up to full size. (One side of the tubing will be flat and the other will remain somewhat convex.) Turn the tubing upside down and flatten the opposite side of the other end. Repeat to flatten the ends of the remaining pieces.

2. Cut an 18" (45.72 cm) piece of 2"-dia. PVC pipe; clamp the first 12" (30.5 cm) of the PVC into a workbench. Clamp one end of a piece of tubing to the end of the PVC pipe with locking pliers. (Make sure the flat side of the tubing is facing the PVC.) Slowly wrap the tubing around the PVC, making almost one complete revolution; take care not to crimp the copper. Remove the tubing, clamp the opposite end to the PVC (again, the flat side of the tubing should face the PVC), and wrap the tubing around the PVC in the same manner. Repeat with each of the nine remaining pieces of tubing.

3. Unwrap the ends of each piece of tubing and refine each piece into an elongated S shape. One end should remain rather tightly curved and the other should be somewhat more open. When you're satisfied with the shape, refine the other pieces, using the first as a pattern.

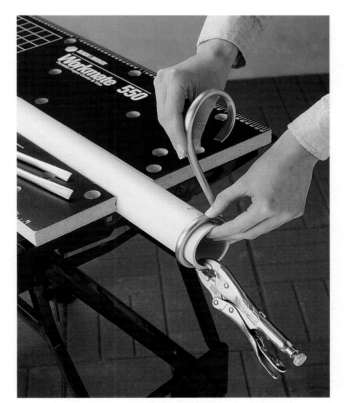

A. *Flatten the ends of ten pieces of copper tubing, and then shape each piece into an S curve.*

B. *Arrange pairs of arms and mark the contact points; mark the apex of each outer curve as well.*

Step B: Mark the Contact Points

1. Draw an 18" (45.72 cm) straight line on a large piece of foamboard. Lay out two S-shaped arms along the line, and adjust the relationship between the arms until they form a pleasing shape. Mark the contact points between each arm and the line, and between the two arms. Also, mark the locations for the candle cups at the apex of the curve of the two outer ends of the tubing.

2. One by one, lay the remaining pairs of arms over the first pair and duplicate the marks.

Step C: Prepare for the Candle Cups

Slide the outer ends of each of the arms back onto the PVC pipe. Centerpunch and drill a ⅛" (3 mm) hole at each mark; drill all the way through the tubing. Remove the arms from the PVC and enlarge the holes on the inside of the curves only, using a ¼" (6.35 mm) bit.

Step D: Connect the Arms

1. Clamp two 6" (15.25 cm) sections of ⅜" copper tubing next to each other in a small bench vise. Cut five 10" (25.4 cm) lengths of 12-gauge copper wire. Wrap each length of wire tightly around the copper tubing at least four times, creating five coils of wire.

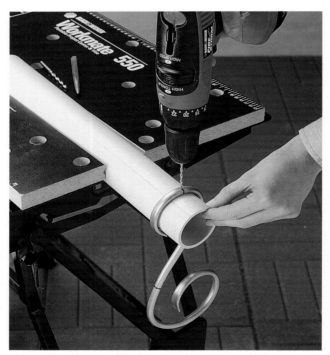

C. *On each arm, slip the outer curve back onto the PVC and drill a hole through the tubing at the cup marks.*

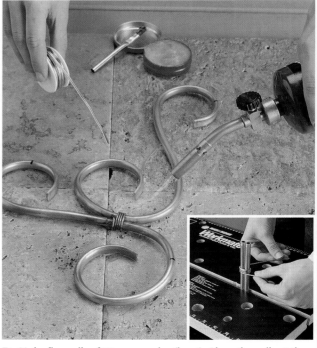

D. *Make five coils of 12-gauge wire (inset). Place the coils at the marked spots and solder the arms together.*

Trim the coils to the same size, using wire nippers.

2. Slip the large ends of two S-shaped arms into a coil. Arrange the arms and align the layout marks you made in Step B. Adjust the coil and flux it thoroughly. Solder the coil in place, making sure it's completely full of solder. (For more information on soldering, see pages 104 to 105.) Repeat to join the remaining four pairs of arms.

Step E: Add Candle Cups

Remove the base portion from ten ¾" standoffs, using channel-type pliers. Thread a 1" 8 × 32 round-head machine screw up through the hole in each arm and through a standoff. Fasten the standoff in place, using a nut.

Step F: Construct the Spacing Jig

1. Draw a line through the center of an 18 × 20" (45.72 × 50.8 cm) piece of foamboard. Mark the center of the line, and use a compass to draw an 8⅜"-dia. (21.27 cm) circle at the center of the foamboard.

2. Using a protractor, draw a line every 72° to divide the circle.

3. Use a utility tool to cut a ¼"-wide (6.35 mm) slot centered over each line.

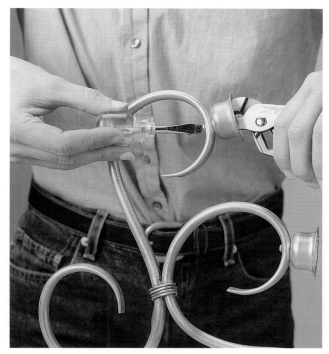

E. *Remove the bases from ten plumbing standoffs. Attach a standoff to each outer curve, using machine screws and nuts.*

F. *Draw an 8⅜"-diameter circle on a piece of foamboard. Equally divide the circle with five lines, and then cut out a ¼" slot along each line.*

G. *Use 1"-dia. PVC pipe as a form to shape an upper retaining ring from 12-gauge wire, and a lower ring from ¼" tubing.*

Step G: Form the Retaining Rings

1. Clamp 12" (30.5 cm) of an 18" (45.72 cm) piece of 1"-dia. PVC tubing into a workbench. Wrap 12-gauge copper wire tightly around the form at least five times. Remove the coil and trim it with a wire nipper. This is the upper retaining ring.

2. Wrap ¼" copper tubing around the PVC three times. (You'll use only the complete circle formed at the center.) Cut through the tubing, using a band saw, to produce a single, slightly offset ring. This is the lower retaining ring.

3. Cut two 1½" (3.8 cm) pieces of ⅜" copper tubing and flare one end of each. These are the spacers.

Step H: Assemble the Chandelier

1. Slip the tops of all five arms into the 12-gauge wire retaining ring. Center the assembly over the

spacing jig and adjust the arms. Tape the arms into position within the spacing jig.

2. Slip one of the spacers into the center of the ring formed at the top of the assembly.

3. Use two pairs of pliers to spread apart the arms of the lower retaining ring. Remove the assembly from the spacing jig, and then slip the second spacer into the center of the ring formed at the bottom of the chandelier. Use a large pair of channel-type pliers to crimp the ring back into a circle. Flux each area thoroughly and solder the spacers in place. Make sure that each retaining ring is saturated with solder.

Step I: Add the Hanging Stem

1. Cut a 30" (76 cm) piece of ¼" copper tubing for the hanging stem. Wrap the first 6" (15.25 cm) of the tubing around the piece of 1"-dia. PVC, forming a slightly elliptical loop. Wrap the joint with 12-gauge copper wire, at least four times. Solder the joint.

2. Straighten the remaining portion of the stem and thread it through both ⅜" spacers in the center of the chandelier. Flare the bottom of the stem, which will lock it in place.

SPACER TUBE DETAIL

Hanging stem

⅜" (9.5 mm) flexible copper tubing

Lower retaining ring

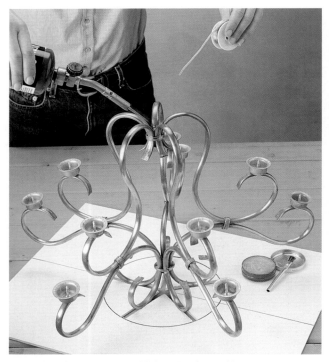

H. *Gather the arms and hold them in place with ⅜" tubing spacers and the retaining rings.*

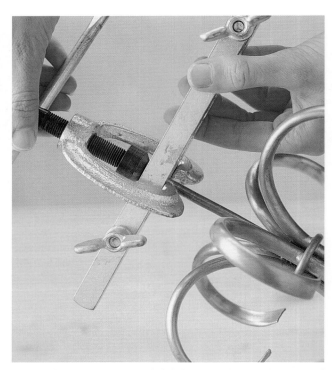

I. *Form the hanging stem and slide it into position at the center of the chandelier. Flare the bottom of the stem to hold it in place.*

Decorative Birdhouse

Birdhouses are popular in garden decorating, both indoors and out. This particular version is strictly decorative—its simple design makes it impractical for actual habitation. In fact, the holes are covered with screen to keep birds from trying to make themselves at home. You could make a habitable version, though—just add floors to subdivide the sections and hinge the back so it can be opened for cleaning.

The tin roof is made from galvanized flashing. It's easy to work with, but the edges are quite sharp—wear heavy gloves when cutting and bending it.

I happen to love the weathered, worn appearance created by the finishing techniques we used here. If you're not fond of that look, skip the stain, wax, and distressing steps—simply paint the lumber. Since the birdhouse is meant to be ornamental rather than functional, you can use any color or combination of colors you like, rather than limiting yourself to colors that attract birds. You could even use some decorative painting techniques to brighten or embellish it, if that suits the style of your garden.

While you can set this birdhouse on a table or other piece of furniture, you might prefer to mount it on a stand. An old newel post from a porch or deck works beautifully for this. Start by toe-nailing the newel post to a base large enough to give it stability. Next, drill a

hole in the bottom of the birdhouse and tap in a T-nut. Install a furniture bolt in the top of the newel post, and then screw the bolt into the nut. Voila!

TOOLS & MATERIALS

- Hammer
- Straightedge
- Circular saw
- Miter box
- Drill and ¼" (6.35 mm) twist bit
- 1" (2.54 cm) spade bit
- Clamps
- Heavy-duty stapler and staples
- Aviation snips
- Heavy-duty awl or flat file
- 1 × 6 (2.54 × 15.25 cm) pine (4 ft. [1.22 m])
- 1 × 1 (2.54 × 2.54 cm) pine (5 ft. [1.5 m])
- 1 × 2 (2.54 × 5 cm) pine (2½ ft. [76.2 cm])

- 2 × 6 (5 × 15.25 cm) pine (at least 5½" [13.97 cm])
- Foam brush
- Exterior wood glue
- 4d (4 cm) finish nails
- 2" (5 cm) deck screws
- Water-based stain
- Beeswax
- Latex paint
- Polyurethane sealer
- Fine wire mesh or screening
- 18-gauge (1.25 mm) galvanized sheet metal (at least 18" [45.72 cm] square)
- Wooden drapery finial
- Heavy gloves

CUTTING LIST

Lumber	Piece	Size
1 × 6	4 (front, back & sides)	21" (53.34 cm)
1 × 1	8 (trim)	7" (17.8 cm)
1 × 2	4 (base trim)	7" (17.8 cm)
2 × 6	1 (roof support)	5½ × 5½" (13.97 × 13.97 cm)

ROOF SHOWN IN CROSS SECTION

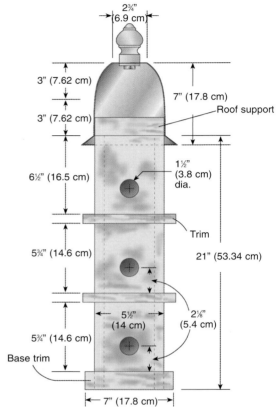

2¾" (6.9 cm)
3" (7.62 cm)
7" (17.8 cm)
Roof support
3" (7.62 cm)
1½" (3.8 cm) dia.
6½" (16.5 cm)
Trim
5¾" (14.6 cm)
21" (53.34 cm)
5½" (14 cm)
2⅛" (5.4 cm)
5¾" (14.6 cm)
Base trim
7" (17.8 cm)

HOW TO BUILD A DECORATIVE BIRDHOUSE

Step A: Assemble the Tower

1. Cut the lumber as indicated on the Cutting List. Rip two side pieces to 4" (10 cm) wide.

2. On the front piece, mark three centerpoints as indicated on the diagram. Drill a hole at each mark, using a 1" spade bit. Lightly sand the faces and edges of each piece, then mark placement lines for the trim pieces.

3. Cut three 2" (5 cm) squares of fine wire mesh or screening. Staple one piece of mesh across the back of each of the holes on the front piece.

4. Spread exterior wood glue along the edges of the front piece, then clamp it to the two side pieces. Nail the front to the sides, using 4d finish nails. When the glue is dry, attach the back piece to the sides, using glue and nails.

5. Cut 45° miters on the ends of the trim pieces. (Each trim piece should be 7" [17.8 cm] long at the long edges of the miter.) Tack these pieces in position at the marked lines, using 4d finish nails.

Step B: Add the Finish

1. Distress the surface of the tower by gouging small holes here and there with an awl.

2. Brush water-based stain over the entire tower assembly, using a foam brush. (We used golden oak.) Let the stain dry overnight.

3. Rub beeswax onto the areas that would natural-

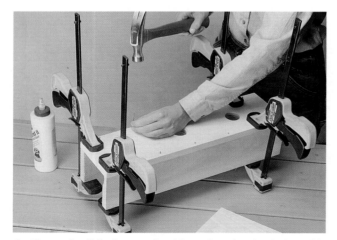

A. *Glue and nail the front to the sides. When the glue is dry, add the back and then the trim.*

ly show wear—around the holes, edges, and sides. Paint the tower assembly. (We used antique white.) The moisture in the paint will lift some of the stain, discoloring the paint and creating a weathered, aged effect. While the paint is still wet, use a clean, dry rag to rub some of it off, especially in the waxed areas. Let the paint dry thoroughly.

4. Apply a coat of polyurethane sealer to the entire tower.

Step C: Prepare the Roof

1. Using the grid system or a photocopier, enlarge the roof pattern shown on page 108. Cut out the pattern, then trace it onto a piece of galvanized sheet metal.

2. Use aviation snips to cut along the outline, then use a straightedge and a heavy-duty awl or the tail of a flat file to score the texture lines. Again using aviation snips, cut along the dotted lines. If necessary, use a rotary tool to smooth the cut edges. Finally, score the metal along the fold lines.

3. Fold down the sides of the roof along the marked, scored fold lines at the top, and then fold the lower edges up at the marked, scored lines.

4. Mark and drill a ¼" (6.35 mm) hole at the center of the roof. Insert a 2" deck screw through the hole in the center of the roof piece, and use it to secure a finial to the top of the roof.

Step D: Install the Roof

1. Set the 2 × 6 roof support on top of the tower assembly and, on each side, drill two angled pilot holes up through the tower and into the roof support. Drive a 2" deck screw into each pilot hole, attaching the roof support to the tower assembly.

2. Line up the folded edge of each side of the roof with the lower edge of the corresponding side of the roof support. Nail the roof to the roof support, using evenly spaced, 4d finish nails.

B. *Distress the wood, then stain, paint, and finish the tower.*

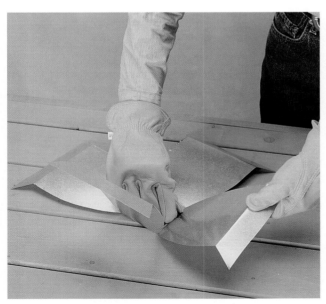

C. *Trace the pattern onto the sheet metal, then cut and shape the tin roof.*

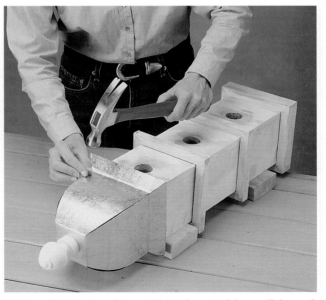

D. *Screw the 2 × 6 roof support into place, and then nail the roof to that support.*

Candle Tree

Imagine the flickering light of dozens of candles dancing with the foliage and flowers in the evening breeze, weaving a magical spell upon the garden. A candle tree is a wonderful way to transform that image into reality. It's so inexpensive and easy to build that you could make several to line a pathway or to light an entertainment area.

A candelabra like this looks great in a container planted with medium-height flowers and trailing foliage. Just insert the stem into the soil and push it down until it's stable. However, to install one in a planting area or other open ground, it's best to provide an anchor. An easy way to do that is to drive a 36" (91.44 cm) piece of rebar about 18" (45.72 cm) into the ground, and then fit the candlelabra's stem over the rebar.

By varying the length of the hanging loops, you can arrange the candle cups at various heights in much the same way you would arrange flowers in a vase. If necessary, adjust the curve of individual branches to create a pleasing arrangement.

A note of caution: Never leave candles burning unattended. And although the candelabra is quite stable when properly installed, it's a good idea to remove the glass candle holders during storms, just to be on the safe side.

TOOLS & MATERIALS

- Locking-style pliers
- Rubber mallet
- Bandsaw or hacksaw and metal-cutting blade
- Pliers (2 pair)
- Ball-peen hammer
- Center punch
- Drill and $\frac{3}{32}$" (2.38 mm) twist bit
- Propane torch
- Aviation snips
- Wire brush
- Tubing cutter
- 8-gauge (4 mm) copper wire
- Anvil
- 5-gallon (19-l) metal bucket
- Flux and flux brush
- Solder
- $\frac{3}{4} \times \frac{1}{2}$" (19.05 × 12.7 mm) reducer coupling
- $\frac{1}{2}$" (12.7 mm) copper pipe (5 ft. [1.5 m])
- $\frac{3}{4}$" (19.05 mm) copper pipe (5" [12.7 cm])
- 16-gauge (1.5 mm) galvanized wire (27 ft. [8.2 m])
- Hot glue gun and glue
- Glass votive holders (9)

HOW TO BUILD A CANDLE TREE

Step A: Curve the Branches

1. Cut 8-gauge copper wire into three 9 ft. (2.74 m) sections. Lay the sections out and mark each every 3 ft. (91.44 cm).

2. Using a locking pliers, clamp a section of wire to a 5-gallon metal bucket and wrap the wire around the bucket. Use a rubber mallet to tap the wire into shape. Repeat with the other sections of wire to produce three coils, approximately 12" (30.5 cm) in diameter.

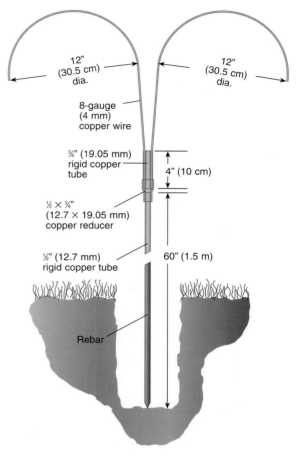

12" (30.5 cm) dia. 12" (30.5 cm) dia.

8-gauge (4 mm) copper wire

$\frac{3}{4}$" (19.05 mm) rigid copper tube

4" (10 cm)

$\frac{1}{2} \times \frac{3}{4}$" (12.7 × 19.05 mm) copper reducer

$\frac{1}{2}$" (12.7 mm) rigid copper tube

60" (1.5 m)

Rebar

Shown in cross-section

A. *Clamp one end of a 9-ft. piece of copper wire to a bucket and form a coil. Cut the coil into 3 ft. sections.*

3. Cut each coil at each mark, using a bandsaw and a metal-cutting blade, if possible. If you don't have a bandsaw, use a hacksaw and a gentle touch.

Step B: Tailor the Branches

1. Mark each of the nine branches, 12" from one end. Straighten each branch, using two pairs of pliers—with one pair of pliers, grip the wire at the 12" mark, and use the other pair to straighten the wire from the mark to the nearest end.

2. On the opposite (still curved) end, flatten the first 1½" (3.8 cm) of the wire, using a ball-peen hammer and an anvil or other durable, flat surface. Continue striking the wire until the end is approximately $\frac{5}{16}$" (8 mm) wide. On each branch, mark, center punch, and drill a $\frac{3}{32}$" (2.38 mm) hole in the center of the flattened area, about $\frac{1}{4}$" (6.35 mm) from the end.

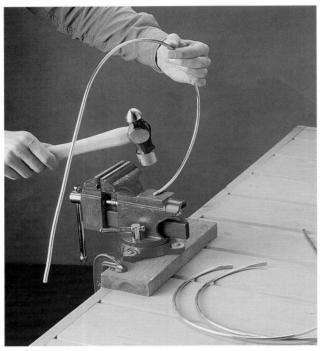

B. *Shape each branch and then use a ball-peen hammer to flatten the curved end. Drill a ³⁄₃₂" hole in each flattened end.*

Step C: Assemble the Branches

1. Clean and flux the first 2" (5 cm) of each branch. Cut a 1" (2.54 cm) piece of ¾" copper pipe to use as a temporary gathering band. (If possible, use a bandsaw to cut this nipple—using a tubing cutter may crimp the pipe.)

2. Slip the straightened ends of eight of the branches into the gathering band, and turn the assembly upside down so the curved portions rest on a level, heat-resistant work surface. Fan the branches out evenly, and then fit the last branch into the band. Position the gathering band 4" (10 cm) from the straightened ends of the branches; make sure the ends are even and that they fit tightly into the band.

3. Using a propane torch, heat a pair of branches and feed a bit of solder between them. Continue this process until all of the branches are connected to one another. Cut the gathering band away, using aviation snips, then clean up the soldered area with a wire brush.

Step D: Complete the Branch Assembly

Slip the soldered end of the assembly into a 4"

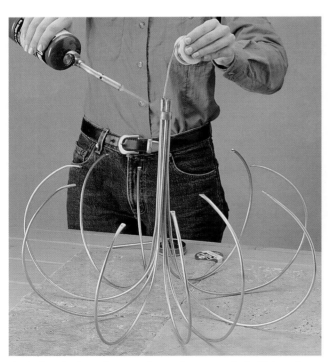

C. *Gather the branches together and temporarily hold them in place with a 1" piece of ¾" copper. Solder the branches together and cut away the gathering band.*

D. *Slide the branch assembly into a 4" piece of ¾" copper pipe. Gently tap it into place with a rubber mallet, if necessary.*

length of ¾" copper pipe. If necessary, use a rubber mallet to tap the assembly into place, but be careful not to distort the shape of the branches. At this point, you can reshape the curves of the branches if you like. The goal is to slightly vary the heights of the branches as you would flowers in a bouquet.

Step E: Add the Base

1. Clean, flux, and solder a ¾ × ½" reducer coupling to one end of a 60" (1.5 m) length of ½" copper pipe.

2. Clean, flux, and solder the branch assembly to the reducer fitting.

Step F: Add the Candle Cups

1. Form an open loop at each end of a 12" (30.5 cm) piece of 16-gauge galvanized wire. Use a dab of hot glue to hold the wire in place at each side of a glass votive holder. Cut a wire about 20" (50.8 cm) long, and wrap it around the votive holder three or four times, securing the hanging wire in position. Tuck the end of the wrapped wire behind the hanging wire and trim it so the loop ends neatly.

2. Cut nine 1¼" (3.2 cm) pieces of 16-gauge wire, and form each into an S-shaped hook. Insert one end of each hook into the hole of a branch, then suspend a votive holder from each.

TIP: MAKE YOUR OWN CANDLES

Tealights work well for this candelabra, but they burn quickly. For longer lasting candles, you can make your own. You'll need glass votive holders, small papercore wick, plastic stir sticks, small wick sustainers, needlenose pliers and paraffin wax.

Prime a length of wick by dipping it into melted wax for a few seconds and then allowing it to dry.

Stick the end of a wick into the hole in a wick sustainer. Use needlenose pliers to crimp the metal around the wick. Tie the other end of the wick to a stir stick, then set the stick across the mouth of the votive holder, centered and as straight as possible.

Melt the paraffin wax over indirect heat, using a double boiler. Heat the wax slowly and watch it closely.

When the wax is melted, carefully pour it into the votive holders, filling each one about ⅔ full. When the wax has cooled and solidified, trim the wicks to extend approximately ⅝" (15.86 mm) above the surface of the candles.

Note: Do not pour melted wax or any clean-up water containing melted wax into a sink. Wax solidifies quickly and will clog the drain.

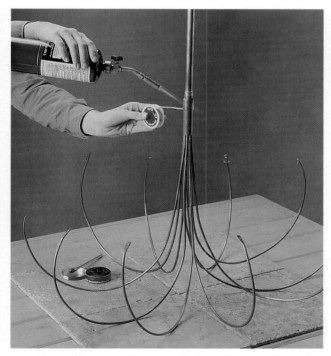

E. *Solder a reducer coupling to a 60" piece of copper pipe, and then to the branch assembly.*

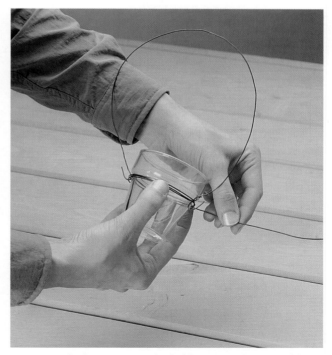

F. *Form a wire loop over a votive holder. Wrap wire around the holder to secure the hanging loop.*

Tealight Candelabra

The vine theme of this candelabra is right at home in a garden. Its shape and scale also make it appropriate for a porch, patio, or deck. Placed slightly behind or to the side of a seating area, it provides a warm glow for summer evening get-togethers. With citronella candles, it might even help keep timid mosquitoes away from the party. (Here in Minnesota, mosquitoes aren't intimidated by citronella candles or much of anything else.)

Don't be intimidated by the shaping of the vine. It's actually really simple if you follow Tim's directions carefully. And, just in case you're not familiar with standoffs, you should know that you'll find them at hardware stores and home centers in areas where other plumbing materials are sold. They're bell-shaped parts that are used to hold plumbing lines away from framing members, such as floor or ceiling joists and wall studs.

TOOLS & MATERIALS

- Channel-type pliers
- Aviation snips
- Tubing cutter
- Rubber mallet
- Locking pliers
- Carpenter's square
- Center punch
- Drill and ³⁄₁₆" (4.76 mm) twist bit
- Flat file
- Compass
- Reciprocating saw or hacksaw
- Propane torch
- Protractor
- Two-part epoxy
- Tealight cups (3)
- ½" (12.7 mm) flexible copper (20 ft. [6 m])

- Clamps
- Foamboard or plywood scrap
- 10-24, ¾" (19.05 cm) brass machine screws and nuts (3)
- ½" (12.7 mm) copper standoffs (3)
- ¼" (6.35 mm) flexible copper tubing (6 ft. [1.82 m])
- 10-gauge (3 mm) copper wire (4 ft. [1.22 m])
- Duct tape
- Flux and flux brush
- Solder
- Toilet flange
- Scrap 2 × 4 (5 × 10 cm)
- 1¼"-dia. (3.2 cm) PVC pipe or dowel (scrap)
- 3½"-dia. (8.9 cm) PVC pipe (scrap)

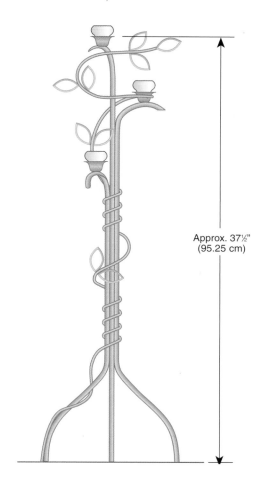

Approx. 37½"
(95.25 cm)

HOW TO BUILD A TEALIGHT CANDELABRA

Step A: Shape the Tops

1. Cut three pieces of ½" flexible copper, 60" (1.5 m), 54" (1.37 m), and 48" (1.22 m). Mark a point 3" (7.62 cm) from one end and another mark 20" (50.8 cm) from the opposite end of each piece. Using a rubber mallet, shape the first 3" (7.62 cm) of each piece of copper; completely flatten the ends and then taper up to the full shape at the 3" mark.

2. Screw a toilet flange to a scrap 2 × 4, and clamp

A. *Clamp flexible copper tubing to a toilet flange and wrap it around the flange, shaping the tops of the candelabra legs.*

B. *Shape the ends of the legs into gradual S curves, then mark the tops of the legs and cut them to shape.*

the 2 × 4 into a workbench. Clamp the flattened end of one piece of copper tubing to the toilet flange, and wrap the pipe around the flange. Work slowly, and be careful not to kink the tubing as you wrap it around the flange. Repeat with the other two pieces.

Step B: Shape the Legs & Trim the Tops

1. Starting at the 20" mark on one of the legs, curve the pipe out and down to form a very gradual S shape. Lay a second leg next to the first, and align the 20" marks. Form an S shape that duplicates the first leg. Repeat to shape the third leg.

2. Lay each of the legs flat on a work surface. Using a carpenter's square, mark a cutting line on the out-

side edge of the curve, directly across from the point at which it intersects the straight portion of the leg. Trim the tubing at an angle, using a reciprocating saw or hacksaw.

Step C: Shape the Vine

Cut a 6 ft.-piece (1.83 m) of ¼" copper tubing. Starting at a point about 18" (45.72 cm) from one end, wrap the tubing around a piece of 1¼" PVC pipe or a dowel; wrap the tubing around the pipe or dowel 5 times. Slide the tubing off the pipe or dowel. Leave 10" (25.4 cm) of the tubing straight, then wrap it around the pipe three more times.

Step D: Join the Legs & Add the Vine

1. Stack the legs, align them with one another, and then slide the coiled tubing onto them.

2. Draw a circle on a scrap of plywood or foam-board, then use a protractor to draw lines that divide the circle every 120°. Arrange the legs so that one foot rests on each line, and then tape the tubing together with duct tape. Apply flux just below the first coil, then solder the legs together.

3. Pull the coiled areas apart and position the tubing in a vine-like arrangement around the candelabra. Solder the vine into place.

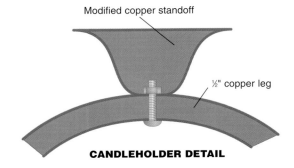

Modified copper standoff

½" copper leg

CANDLEHOLDER DETAIL

C. *Wrap ¼" tubing around a piece of 1¼"-diameter PVC pipe to shape the vine.*

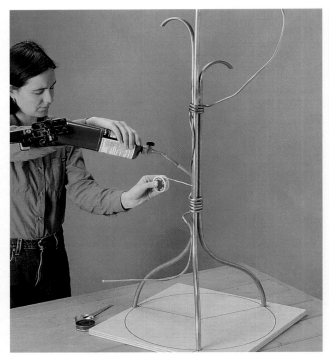

D. *Slide the vine onto the legs, then arrange the legs so that they're 120° apart. Solder the legs together and arrange the position of the vine.*

Step E: Shape the Leaves

1. Cut a 45" (1.14 m) piece of 10-gauge copper wire. Along the length of the wire, make a red mark every 5" (12.7 cm) and a black mark every 2½" (6.35 cm).

2. Clamp the end of the wire around a scrap of 3½"-dia. PVC pipe; wrap the wire around the pipe tightly. Remove the coil from the pipe, pulling the coils apart. Snip the wire at each black mark, using aviation snips. At each red mark, crimp the wire; bend each piece of wire into a leaf shape.

Step F: Embellish the Vine

Tailor the ends of each leaf with a flat file or a grindstone so that the ends are flat. Flux the wire and tubing, and solder each leaf into place.

Step G: Add the Candleholders

1. Remove the base portion from three ½" standoffs, using channel-type pliers.

2. Mark, center-punch, and drill a ¾₆" (4.76 mm) hole at the apex of the curve at the top of each leg. Insert a machine screw from a standoff up through the hole and into the cup. From the top, add a nut to secure the standoff to the tubing.

3. Attach one tealight cup onto each standoff, using two-part epoxy.

E. *Coil 10-gauge copper wire around a scrap of 3½"-diameter PVC pipe, and cut the wire into 5" pieces. Shape each piece into a leaf.*

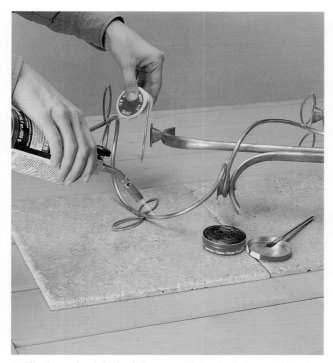

F. *File the ends of the leaf shapes until they're flat enough to sit squarely on the vine. Flux the leaves and the tubing, and solder each leaf in place.*

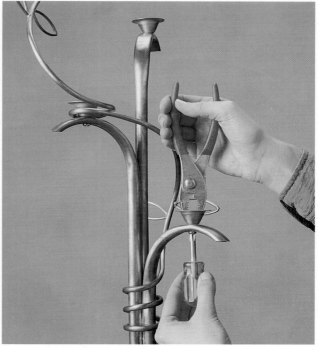

G. *Drill a hole at the apex of the curve on the top of each leg. Disassemble three plumbing standoffs and secure each to a leg, using a machine screw and nut.*

Carved Stones

Carved stones give voice to a garden. They can express welcome, encouraging words—even humor. One easy way to carve stones involves using a rotary tool and diamond-tipped bit. The equipment, which is available at hobby and home improvement stores, costs approximately $40 to 50. We've carved dozens of stones with only a small handful of bits.

We've had tremendous fun scattering carved stones along walking paths, in parks, and other public places. We typically place them in slightly unusual spots, where only observant folks with sharp eyes will see them. We've also found that personalized carved stones are warmly received gifts. We like to surprise people with clever messages or unusual symbols.

On-line, internet sites can be a good place to find designs. There are sites dedicated to Native American and Celtic hieroglyphs, or Asian language symbols. It's best to avoid intricate designs that would be difficult to follow with the rotary tool.

The best stones for carving have even coloration, a relatively smooth texture, and flat or uniformly rounded surfaces. Crystalline rocks, such as quartz or granite, are somewhat difficult to carve, but if you're patient, the results can be spectacular. Dark stones work well because the interior layer revealed by the bit usually contrasts well with the surface.

When carving, set the rotary tool at a fairly high speed at first. Higher speeds generally work the best, though this does vary with the type of stone. You may have to experiment a bit—some stones may carve best at slightly slower speeds.

TOOLS & MATERIALS

- Stones
- Variable-speed rotary tool
- Diamond bits
- Transfer paper (sold at fabric stores)
- Stylus
- Particle mask
- Safety goggles
- Artist's brush
- High-gloss enamel or permanent marker

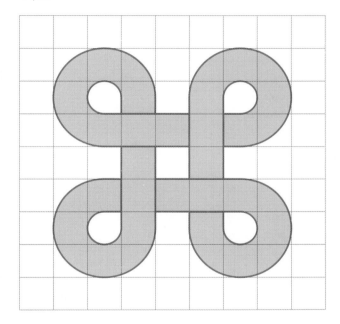

HOW TO MAKE CARVED STONES

Step A: Transfer the Design

Copy or trace the design, and then use transfer paper and a stylus or other gently pointed tool to reproduce the design on the stone.

Step B: Carve the Design

1. Gently score a preliminary groove along the lines of the design, using very light hand pressure with a rotary tool and a diamond bit. Wear safety goggles and a particle mask. It's best to clamp small stones in a vise or workbench while you carve.

2. Retrace the lines until the grooves are deep enough. Never force the tool into the stone, which would overtax the motor and dull the cutting bit.

Step C: Highlight the Carving

1. Wash the stone with mild soap and water and let it dry.

2. Using a fine artist's brush, apply a high-gloss enamel to the carved area. Or, use a permanent marker to highlight the carving.

A. *Transfer the design or words to the surface of the stone, using transfer paper and a stylus or gently pointed tool.*

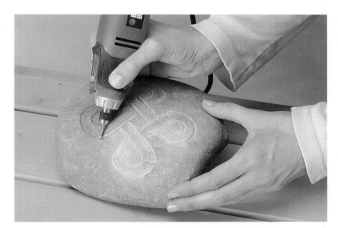

B. *Follow the lines of the design with the rotary tool, using a light touch. Retrace the lines until they're clearly visible.*

C. *Paint the grooves with high-gloss enamel to emphasize the contrast between the design and the stone.*

Door Spring Bug

Put away the pesticide. These bugs are not just adorable—they're useful, too: Flying at the top of a metal rod, they can be put to work as plant stakes.

The bug shown below sat in a friend's garden through one winter and one summer before we photographed it—just enough time to develop a lovely layer of rust and character. If you prefer a clean, crisp look, spray your bug with a coat of polyurethane sealer before putting it outside.

TOOLS & MATERIALS

- Drill and ¼" (6.35 mm) and ³⁄₁₆" (4.76 mm) twist bits
- Aviation snips
- Propane torch
- Flat file
- Hot glue gun
- ½" (12.7 mm) threaded flare plug
- 10-32 knurled nut, brass
- 10-32 × 1" (2.54 cm) slotted roundhead machine screw, brass
- ¼"-dia. (6.35 mm) extension spring
- Center punch
- Wire stripper
- Flux and flux brush
- Solder
- Spring-style door stopper, antique brass
- ³⁄₈" (9.5 mm) glass beads (3)
- Glass seed beads (6)
- 12-gauge (2 mm) copper wire
- ³⁄₈" (9.5 mm) brass tube
- ¼" (6.35 mm) rod (36" [91.44 cm])
- Bell wire

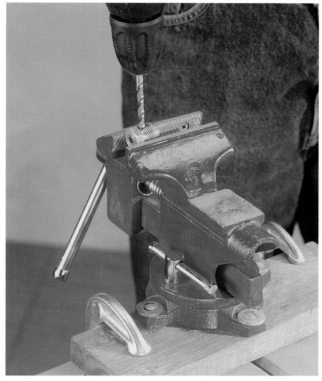

A. *Center-punch and drill two ¼" holes in a ½" threaded flare plug—one hole in the center of the flat cap end and one in the body of the plug.*

HOW TO BUILD A DOOR SPRING BUG
Step A: Construct the Body

1. Mark and centerpunch holes on a ½" threaded flare plug, one in the center of the flat cap end and one in the center of the main body of the plug. Drill ¼" (6 mm) holes at each of these locations.

2. Using aviation snips, cut away the loop from one end of ¼" extension spring. Insert the remaining loop end of the spring into the ¼" hole in the center of the body.

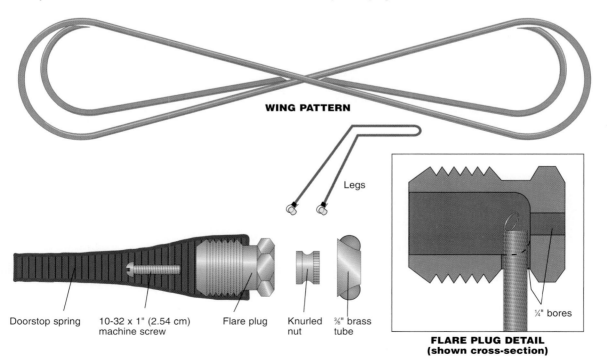

WING PATTERN

Legs

Doorstop spring | 10-32 x 1" (2.54 cm) machine screw | Flare plug | Knurled nut | ³⁄₈" brass tube

¼" bores

FLARE PLUG DETAIL
(shown cross-section)

Step B: Assemble the Body

Thread a 10-32 × 1" machine screw into the open end of the flare plug, through the spring loop, and through the ¼" hole at the end of the plug. Lock this screw in place with a 10-32 knurled nut.

Step C: Add the Wings

1. Following the diagram on page 71, shape the legs and wings from 12-gauge copper wire.

2. Flux the contact points and solder the wings to the top of the flare-plug body.

Step D: Add the Stem & Legs

1. Thread a spring-style door stopper onto the threaded end of the flare plug.

2. Flux the contact points and solder the legs to the bottom of the flare-plug body.

Step E: Construct the Head

1. Use a flat file to shape a bevel on the end of a 2" (5 cm) piece of ⅜" brass tube.

2. On the long side of the bevel, mark a point ⅜" (9.5 mm) from the end of the tube, and then center-punch and drill a ³⁄₁₆" hole.

3. Mark the tube at a point ¾" (19.05 mm) from the long side of the bevel, and cut the tube to length. Bevel this end of the tube, again using a flat file.

Step F: Assemble the Head

Shape the antenna from 12-gauge copper wire. Flux the contact points and solder them to the top of the ⅜"-tube head.

Step G: Embellish the Bug

1. Strip some bell wire and cut six 2" (5 cm) lengths. Wrap each piece around a length of 12-gauge wire to form tight coils with ¼" (6.35 mm) tails. Thread a glass seed bead onto the tail of each coil, and bend the wire down to secure the bead.

2. Trim the legs and antenna to final lengths and add a beaded coil to each.

3. Thread the head onto the end of the machine screw at the cap end of the body. (Be careful not to overtighten it.) For eyes, hot-glue ⅜" glass beads into the open ends of the head, and then glue a bead to the open end of the spring to complete the tail.

4. Insert a 36"-long ¼" rod into the open end of the spring at the bottom of the bug.

B. *Insert a ¼" extension spring into the hole in the body of the flare plug. Thread a machine screw through the spring's loop and then through the hole in the end of the plug. Secure the screw with a knurled nut.*

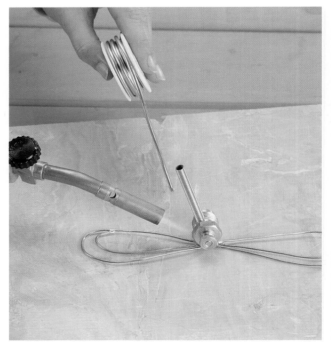

C. *Shape 12-gauge copper wire into wings and legs, and solder these wire shapes to the flare-plug body.*

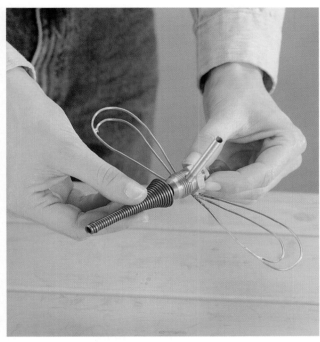

D. *Thread a spring-style door stopper onto the threaded end of the flare plug.*

E. *File a bevel at one end of a piece of ⅜" brass tube. Drill a hole ⅜" from the long side of the bevel, and cut the tube to length. File a bevel at the cut end of the tube to complete the shape of the head.*

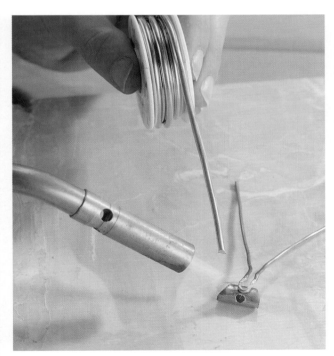

F. *Solder the antennae to the top of the brass-tubing head.*

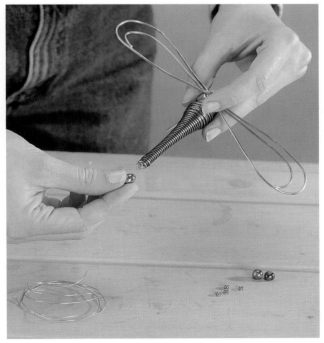

G. *Hot-glue beaded coils to the legs and antennae. Attach two larger beads to the brass-tube head for the eyes and one to the end of the tail.*

Furnishings

When we began thinking of our yards as extensions of our homes, we radically revised our ideas about garden furnishings. Where once the standard may have been limited to a lounge chair and a picnic or other dining table, we've come to understand that well-furnished outdoor homes are more likely to be used and enjoyed. Seating, planters, and display pieces all play important parts in creating a comfortable and appealing atmosphere.

There's no reason to confine your furnishings to the deck or patio. Set a pergola in the middle of a rose garden or amidst a patch of wildflowers in the back corner of the yard. Add a couple of chairs and a small table, and you've created an outdoor breakfast nook or a special place for tea on leisurely afternoons. Or, suspend a swing beneath an elevated deck. Accessorize it with soft cushions, and place candles nearby to produce a gracious spot to relax at the end of a day.

You may have specific ideas about the furnishings you need or want to add to your garden. If not, invest some time in the garden, just thinking about the possibilities. Slow down, use your imagination, and make a plan. Then you'll be ready to build or acquire furnishings that work for the way you live. Or perhaps for the way you want to live.

IN THIS CHAPTER:

Birdhouse Plant Stand

Walk the aisles of any garden center, and you're bound to recognize how popular container gardening has become—there are literally hundreds of types and sizes of containers on the market. One of the many reasons is that container gardens can make the most of small spaces or create a feeling of intimacy in open areas. And in either case, a plant stand can help by providing a place to store and display container plants.

This plant stand also would be a charming addition to a patio, deck, or garden shed. Although they're very easy to produce, details like the shaped

skirting, spindle supports on the shelves, and the birdhouse effect on the posts give it plenty of personality. And while we did a simple colorwashed finish on ours, you could use any paint or stain treatment that complements the style and tone of your yard.

By the way, dollhouse shingles might seem fragile, but the ones I used on the posts of a garden bench now have survived ten years in the unforgiving climate of Minnesota. If you give the whole piece a coat of sealer/preservative every year or so, it should stand up to nearly any weather.

TOOLS & MATERIALS

- Drill with ¼" (6.35 mm) twist bit
- 1" (2.54 cm) spade bit
- Carpenter's square
- Reciprocating or circular saw
- Bar clamps
- Level
- Jig saw
- Ratchet wrench
- Caulk gun
- 8 ft. (2.44 m) cedar 4 × 4 (10 × 10 cm) (1)
- 10 ft. (3 m) cedar 2 × 4 (5 × 10 cm) (3)
- 8 ft. (2.44 m) cedar 1 × 4 (2.5 × 10 cm) (5)
- 8 ft. (2.44 m) cedar 1 × 3 (2.54 × 7.62 cm) (5)
- ¼" (6.35 mm) exterior plywood

- Cedar deck balusters (2)
- Latex paint
- Latex glaze
- 2½" (6.35 cm) deck screws
- 6" (15.25 cm) lag screws
- Exterior wood glue
- 6d (5 cm) finish nails
- 1½" (3.8 cm) deck screws
- 2" (5 cm) deck screws
- 8d (6.4 cm) finish nails
- 1"-dia. (2.54 cm) flexible PVC pipe (54" [1.37 m])
- Dollhouse shingles, cedar
- Construction adhesive
- ¼" (6.35 mm) dowel
- Polyurethane sealer

CUTTING LIST

Part	Lumber	No.	Size
Back supports	4 × 4	2	48" (1.22 m)
Shelf frame fronts & backs	2 × 4	4	42" (1.07 m)
Upper shelf sides	2 × 4	2	16" (40.64 cm)
Upper middle brace	2 × 4	1	13" (33.02 cm)
Lower shelf sides	2 × 4	2	20" (50.8 cm)
Lower middle brace	2 × 4	1	17" (43.18 cm)
Front legs	2 × 4	2	20" (50.8 cm)
Skirting front	¼" plywood	1	5½" × 45½" (13.97 cm × 1.16 m)
Upper side skirt	¼" plywood	2	5½ × 16" (13.97 × 40.64 cm)
Lower side skirt	¼" plywood	2	5½ × 20" (13.97 × 50.8 cm)
Decking	1 × 4	9	46½" (1.18 m)
Pickets	1 × 3	10	36" (91.44 cm)
Roofs	¼" plywood	2	4 × 4" (10 × 10 cm)
		2	4 × 4½" (10 × 11.43 cm)

HOW TO BUILD A BIRDHOUSE PLANT STAND
Step A: Prepare the Lumber

1. Cut the parts as indicated on the cutting list above. On each of the 4 × 4 posts (the back supports), center one mark 3½" (8.9 cm) and then another 5½" (13.97 cm) from the end. Use a 1" spade bit to drill a 1½"-deep (3.8 cm) hole at the top mark, and then a ¼" twist bit to drill a ½"-deep hole at the bottom.

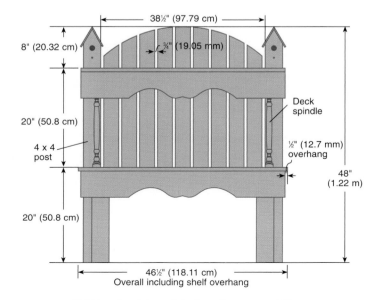

38½" (97.79 cm)
8" (20.32 cm)
¾" (19.05 mm)
Deck spindle
20" (50.8 cm)
½" (12.7 mm) overhang
4 x 4 post
48" (1.22 m)
20" (50.8 cm)
46½" (118.11 cm)
Overall including shelf overhang

Skirting front template found on page 108

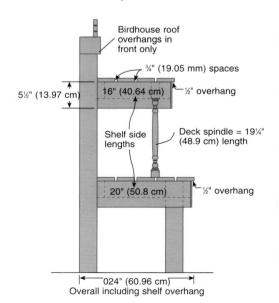

Birdhouse roof overhangs in front only
¾" (19.05 mm) spaces
5½" (13.97 cm)
16" (40.64 cm)
½" overhang
Shelf side lengths
Deck spindle = 19¼" (48.9 cm) length
20" (50.8 cm)
½" overhang
024" (60.96 cm)
Overall including shelf overhang

A. *Drill two holes in the face of each back support, then mark and cut the angles for the roof details.*

2. On the top edge of each post, mark the center, and then on each side mark a point 3" (7.6 cm) down from the top. Draw diagonal lines to connect the marks. Cut along each marked line, using a reciprocating or circular saw.

3. Using the grid system or a photocopier, enlarge the pattern on page 108 and trace it onto the two pieces of ¼" plywood skirting. Cut along the marked lines, using a jig saw.

4. Mix paint and glaze in a 2:1 ratio and use it to wash all the pieces with color.

Step B: Construct the Shelf Frames

1. On a flat, level work surface, lay out the front, back, middle brace, and sides of the upper shelf frame. Drill pilot holes and secure the joints with 2½" deck screws. Repeat with the lower shelf frame.

2. Attach the front legs at the outside corners of the lower shelf frame, using two 2½" deck screws for each leg.

Step C: Attach the Shelf Frames to the Posts

1. On each 4 × 4 back support, mark one line 19¼" (48.9 cm) and another 39¼" (99.7 cm) from the bottom of the post.

2. Clamp the lower shelf frame to the back supports, aligning the top of the frame with the 19¼" marks. On each side, drill two ¼" pilot holes through the frame and into the post; countersink each ¼"

B. *Construct the upper and lower shelf frames. Attach the front legs to the outside corners of the lower shelf frame.*

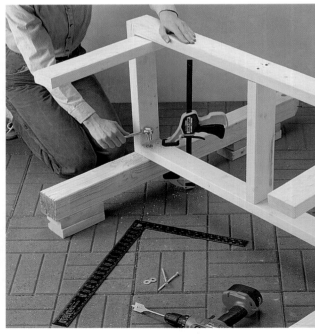

C. *Attach the shelf frames to the back supports, using lag screws and a ratchet wrench.*

deep, using a 1" spade bit. Insert a 4" lag screw and tighten it with a ratchet wrench.

3. Attach the upper shelf frame at the 40" mark.

Step D: Complete the Shelves

1. Apply exterior wood glue to the backs of the skirting pieces and clamp them in place along the sides and front of each shelf frame. (Make sure the top of the skirting is flush with the top of the shelf frame.) Drive a 6d finish nail every couple of inches (5 cm) to secure the skirting to the sides and front.

2. Starting at the back of the frame, add the decking. Drill pilot holes and attach the decking with two 1½" deck screws at each side and at the middle brace. Note: The decking should overhang the ends and the front of the frame by ½" (12.7 mm).

3. Cut two deck balusters to 19¼", trimming an equal amount from each end. Clamp a baluster into position at one outside corner of the upper shelf; use a level to check adjacent sides of the baluster, and adjust until the baluster is plumb. Attach the top of the baluster to the front of the shelf frame, using two 2" deck screws. On the bottom, toenail two sides of the baluster to the decking, using one 6d finish nail on each side of the baluster.

Step E: Add the Details

1. Mark the centers of the upper and lower shelf. Also mark a line down the center of one picket.

Position the picket at the back of the plant stand, flush with the bottom edge of the lower shelf frame and all center marks matching. Drill pilot holes and attach the picket, using 1½" deck screws. Add the remaining pickets, spacing them ¾" (19.05 mm) apart.

2. On the outside edge of the last picket on each side, mark a point 3½" (8.9 cm) above the decking. At the center mark on the center picket, mark another point 8½" (21.6 cm) above the decking. Tack a nail at each of these marks.

3. Cut a 54" (1.37 m) piece of flexible PVC pipe, and clamp it in place at each nail. Adjust the PVC until it creates a pleasing curve. Trace the curve, remove the PVC and nails, and then cut along the marked line, using a jig saw.

4. Spread the top of a post with exterior wood glue and position the plywood roof pieces. Nail the pieces to one another at the peak, and then nail them into the post in the field. Repeat on the other post. On each roof, add rows of dollhouse shingles, securing the shingles with construction adhesive.

5. Cut two 2" pieces of ¼" dowel, and glue one dowel into the small hole in each post.

6. Sand the cut edges of the pickets and touch up the finish. Apply a coat of polyurethane sealer to all surfaces, especially any exposed cut edges.

D. *Glue and nail the skirting in place, then install the decking. Attach the top of the balusters to the sides of the upper shelf frame.*

E. *Add the pickets and trim them to shape. Nail the roof sheathing to the posts, and then add dollhouse shingles.*

Twig & Slat Bench

There are few things more important to a garden than really comfortable benches. Most of us think of benches in terms of providing places for visitors to rest. While that's true, it's only part of the story. The rest is that we, the gardeners, need places to rest, reflect, and take stock of our successes and our challenges. Place benches for your own pleasure and visitors are bound to enjoy them as well.

This bench combines the rustic appeal of branches with the more refined appearance of pickets. Because both trees and fences are common garden elements, the bench looks perfectly natural there.

We liked the contrast of crisp paint against the rough branches, but you might prefer to use an aging technique, such as crackling, a rubbed finish, or pickling on the painted portion of the bench.

TOOLS & MATERIALS

- Loppers
- Jig saw
- Drill
- C clamps (2)
- Strap or bar clamp
- Level
- Branches
- 3½" (8.9 cm) deck screws

- Water-resistant sealer
- 2½" (6.35 cm) deck screws
- 1¼" (3.2 cm) deck screws
- 1½" (3.8 cm) deck screws
- 1 × 4 (2.54 × 10 cm) cedar lumber
- 1 × 6 (2.54 × 15.25 cm) cedar
- Exterior latex paint and brushes

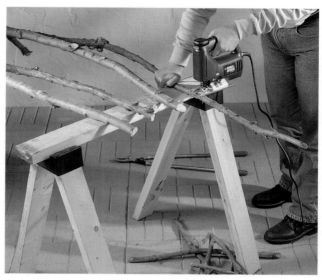

A. Gather branches and cut them to size. Cut the remaining pieces from 1 × 4 and 1 × 6 cedar.

CUTTING LIST

Branches	No.	Size
Legs	4	16¼" (41.28 cm)
Leg Braces	2	19" (48.26 cm)
Center Stretcher	1	35" (88.9 cm)
Upper Back Brace	1	40" (1.02 m)
Side Back Braces	2	22¼" (56.51 cm)
Arm Braces	2	10½" (26.67 cm)
Arms	2	18" (45.72 cm)
1 × 4 Cedar		
Front & Back Seat Braces	3	36½" (92.71 cm)
Side & Center Seat Braces	3	17½" (44.45 cm)
Pickets	7	21½" (54.61 cm)
Corner Braces	4	10¾" (27.30 cm)
1 × 6 Cedar		
Decking	4	40" (1.02 m)

HOW TO BUILD A TWIG & SLAT BENCH
Step A: Gather & Prepare the Branches

1. Cut a supply of branches about 3" (7.6 cm) in diameter. You'll need one branch 6 ft. (1.83 m) long, one branch 5 ft. (1.5 m) long, and nine branches 3 ft. (91.44 cm) long. Remove any twigs and small branches, using loppers.

2. Following the cutting list, cut the pieces to size. When cutting branches, use a jig saw and make your cuts as square as possible. Shape the tops of the pickets as desired.

3. Paint the pieces cut from 1 × 4 cedar.

SEAT CORNER BRACE DETAIL

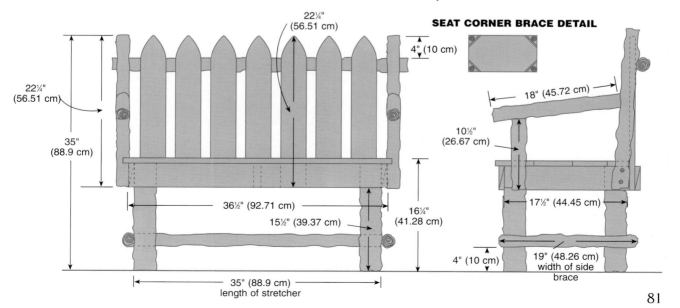

Step B: Construct the Seat

1. Lay out a pair of leg branches on a work surface. Position a brace across the legs, 4" (10 cm) from the bottom and centered horizontally. Holding this brace firmly in place, drill pilot holes through each end and into the legs. Secure each joint with a 2½" deck screw. Repeat this process to construct a second pair of legs.

2. Drill pilot holes and use 2½" deck screws to attach a side seat brace to each leg assembly. Align

the top of the brace with the tops of the legs.

3. Place a pair of legs at either end of a front seat brace. Use two pairs of 2½" deck screws to attach the front brace to each leg assembly—drive one pair of screws into the leg and one pair into the side brace. Repeat to add a back seat brace to the assembly.

4. At the center of the seat assembly, attach the center seat brace, using a pair of 2½" deck screws at the front and at the back.

5. Center the center stretcher between the side leg braces, drill pilot holes and secure the brace with 3½" deck screws.

6. Cut four corner braces, mitering each end at 45°. Position one brace across each corner, and toenail it into place, using 1¼" deck screws.

Step C: Level the Legs

Place the base on a level floor and set a level across the seat. Shim the legs until the seat is level. Using a straight scrap of a 2 × 4, scribe each leg and then trim each, taking care to make square cuts.

Step D: Add the Bench Back

1. Starting 1½" (3.8 cm) from one edge and leaving 1½" between them, attach the pickets to the back brace, using 1¼" deck screws. The ends of the pickets should be flush with the lower edge of the back brace.

2. Clamp the brace and pickets into place. The bottom of the back brace should be flush with the bottom of the seat brace. Attach the back to the seat by driving screws through the back brace and into the seat brace.

B. *Join pairs of legs with braces, and assemble the seat frame. Add the center brace and corner braces.*

C. *Shim the seat until it's level, then mark and trim the legs.*

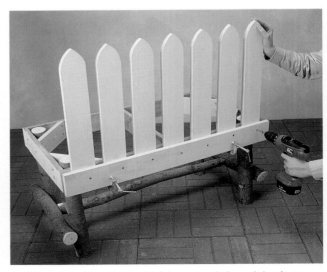

D. *Attach the pickets to the back brace, and clamp it in place. Secure the back brace to the back seat brace.*

Step E: Attach the Bench Back Braces

1. Drill pilot holes and attach the side back braces to the upper back brace, using 2½" deck screws. The top ends of the side braces should extend 4" (10 cm) past the upper back brace.

2. Clamp or band the brace assembly into position, with the top of the upper brace approximately 4" from the tops of the pickets. Drill pilot holes and drive 3½" deck screws through the side braces and into the lower back brace, three screws for each side brace.

3. Attach each picket to the upper back brace, using a pair of 1½" deck screws for each.

Step F: Attach the Arms

1. Cut two arm braces. Drill pilot holes and attach one brace on each side of the seat assembly, using 3½" deck screws. Position the branches so the bottom of each is flush with the lower edge of the side brace.

2. Cut two arms 18" (45.72 cm) long. Position each arm against the side back brace and arm brace, drill pilot holes and attach with 3½" screws.

Step G: Add the Decking & Finish the Bench

1. Measure the side seat braces and notch the ends of a decking board to accommodate them. Attach the board to the seat assembly by driving a pair of 1½" deck screws into each side brace as well as the center brace. Attach two more decking boards. Trim the final decking board, if necessary. Measure the arm braces, notch the ends, and attach them in the same manner.

2. Touch up the painted portion of the bench if necessary, and put a coat of water-resistant sealer on the branches, especially on the cut ends.

E. *Attach the side back braces to the upper back brace. Clamp this assembly into position and secure it to the lower back brace. Drill pilot holes and use pairs of screws to connect each picket to the upper back brace.*

F. *Attach the arm braces at the front of the seat, and then add the arms.*

G. *Notch each end of the first decking board and install it. Add two more boards, then trim, notch, and install the final decking board to fit.*

Porch Swing

When the siren song of privacy lured families to backyard decks, we all lost something important. Back when we played out our day-to-day activities in full view of whomever happened to be on the front porch next door, we forged close connections with our neighbors. Even now, porches and porch swings conjure up images of first dates and furtive good-night kisses, frosty glasses of lemonade, and waiting for the mail. It's easy to imagine that this swing recently held a grandmother piecing a quilt or a teenaged-girl in pincurls, killing time while her nails dried.

Like millions of other people, I live in a suburban house with a modest front entry and an enormous deck in the backyard. But lately, every time I see a great porch, I promise myself that someday I'll have a deep, sprawling porch of my own and that a swing like this will be my port-of-call on sultry summer evenings.

If you're fortunate enough to have a porch or other place to hang a swing, build one and let it remind you to take time to watch the world go by. Maybe even talk with the neighbors.

TOOLS & MATERIALS

- Circular saw
- Router and chamfer bit
- Drill with ³⁄₁₆" (4.76 mm) twist bit and ⅝" (15.86 mm) spade bit
- Hammer
- Chisel
- Jig saw
- Belt sander
- 48" (1.22 m) flexible straightedge
- 1 × 6 (2.54 × 15.25 cm), 8 ft. (2.44 m) (4)
- 1 × 4 (2.54 × 10 cm), 8 ft. (2.44 m) (8)
- 1 × 2 (2.54 × 5 cm), 8 ft. (2.44 m) (2)
- Latex paint

- Latex paint glaze
- Polyurethane sealer
- Paint brushes
- 3" (7.62 cm) galvanized deck screws
- 1½" (3.8 cm) galvanized deck screws
- 2" (5 cm) galvanized deck screws
- Deck balusters (2)
- Exterior wood glue
- C-clamps (2)
- Eye-bolts, nuts and washers
- Heavy chain, 32 ft. (9.75 m)
- 2" (5 cm) connecting links (4)

CUTTING LIST

Key	Part	Lumber	No.	Size
A	Seat support	1 × 6	2	37³⁄₁₆" (94.46 cm)
B	Front cross brace	1 × 6	1	36" (91.44 cm)
C	Rear cross brace	1 × 6	1	36" (91.44 cm)
D	Narrow seat slats	1 × 2	4	37½" (95.25 cm)
E	Wide seat slats	1 × 4	3	37½" (95.25 cm)
F	Center seat brace	1 × 4	1	15½" (39.37 cm)
G	Seat stretcher	1 × 4	1	37½" (95.25 cm)
H	Upper back brace	1 × 4	1	30" (76 cm)
I	Middle back brace	1 × 4	1	37¾" (95.88 cm)
J	Lower back brace	1 × 4	1	36" (91.44 cm)
K	Back slats	1 × 4	8	38" (96.52 cm)
L	Back support	1 × 4	1	44¾" (1.14 m)
M	Arms	1 × 6	2	29¾" (75.57 cm)
N	Arm facings	1 × 4	2	13¾" (34.93 cm)
O	Front arm support	1 × 6	2	15" (38.1 cm)
P	Rear arm support	1 × 6	2	26" (66 cm)

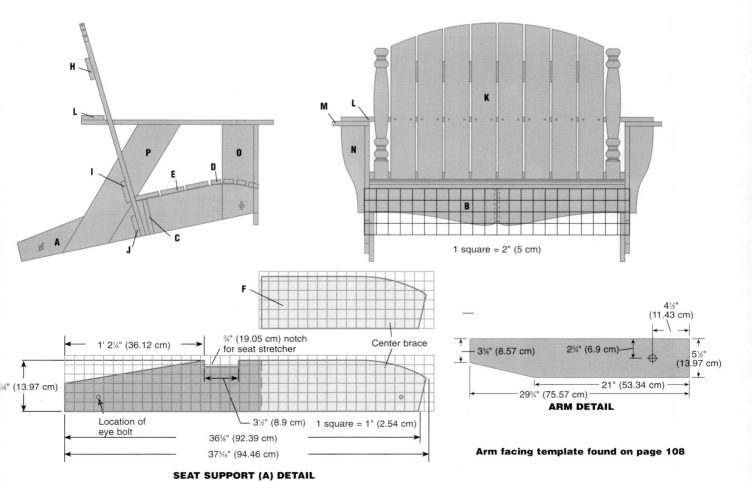

1 square = 2" (5 cm)

SEAT SUPPORT (A) DETAIL

1' 2¼" (36.12 cm)

¾" (19.05 cm) notch for seat stretcher

Center brace

F

Location of eye bolt

3½" (8.9 cm)

1 square = 1" (2.54 cm)

36⅜" (92.39 cm)

37³⁄₁₆" (94.46 cm)

½" (13.97 cm)

ARM DETAIL

4½" (11.43 cm)

3⅜" (8.57 cm)

2¾" (6.9 cm)

5½" (13.97 cm)

21" (53.34 cm)

29¾" (75.57 cm)

Arm facing template found on page 108

HOW TO BUILD A PORCH SWING
Step A: Prepare the Lumber

1. Cut the parts to length, as indicated on the cutting list. Using a router and a chamfer bit, chamfer the edges of all pieces, except those that require further shaping (the seat support, front cross brace, arms, and arm facings).

2. Mix paint and glaze in a 2:1 ratio and use it to wash all the pieces with color.

Step B: Shape the Pieces of the Seat Frame

1. Using the grid system or a photocopier, enlarge the shaping templates on page 85.

2. Trace the proper contour onto one of the seat supports (A), then cut along the cutting lines, using a jig saw. Use this piece as a template to mark and cut an identical seat support. Chamfer the edges and lightly sand each piece.

3. Transfer the placement marks for the front and rear cross braces onto the seat supports as indicated on the seat support template. Also mark the cutting lines for the mortise for the seat stretcher.

4. Set the depth gauge on a circular saw, and then make ¾"-deep (19.05 mm) cuts along each of the cutting lines marked for the mortise. Make an additional cut every ¼" (6.35 mm) between those lines. Remove the waste material, using a hammer and chisel.

5. Trace the proper contour onto the front cross brace (B), and cut it to shape, using a jig saw. Chamfer the edges and lightly sand the piece.

Step C: Build the Seat Frame

1. Align the front cross brace with the placement marks, and attach it between the seat supports, using glue and 3" deck screws. The tops of the pieces must be flush with one another.

2. Position the rear cross brace (C) between the seat supports, aligned with the placement marks; attach the seat support with glue and 3" deck screws. Again, make sure the tops are flush.

3. Using the seat support template on page 85, shape the center seat brace (F). Position the brace in the center of the seat and attach it to the front and

A. *Cut the lumber for the swing, and chamfer the edges of all the slats and arm pieces.*

B. *Contour, shape, and sand two identical seat supports. Cut the mortises for the seat stretcher.*

rear cross braces, using counterbored 1½" deck screws.

4. Set the seat stretcher (G) into position in the mortises. Join these pieces, using a pair of 1½" deck screws on each side.

5. Arrange the seat slats on top of this assembly, using wood scraps to set ⅜" (9.5 mm) spaces between the slats. Start with the four 1 × 2 slats (D), and then add three 1 × 4 slats (E). The first slat should overhang the front of the frame by about ¾" (19.05 cm). Drill counterbored pilot holes and drive 2" deck screws through the holes and into each of the seat supports as well as the center brace.

Step D: Construct the Seat Back

1. Trim two deck balusters to 26¾" (67.94 cm), and round the top of each one, using a belt sander.

2. Gang the back slats together and mark a straight line 22½" (57.15 cm) from the bottom of the slats.

3. Mark the centers of the upper (H), middle (I), and lower (J) back braces. Set the lower and middle braces on a flat surface with the center marks matching and 1" (2.54 cm) of space between them. Position the balusters and back slats (K) on top of the braces, maintaining ½" (12.7 mm) spaces between them. Slide the upper brace into place beneath the slats, aligning it with the line marked across them. Make sure the ends of the slats are flush with the bottom edge of the lower back brace and that their tops remain straight.

4. Drill pilot holes and attach the balusters and slats to the braces, using a pair of 1½" deck screws on each slat for each brace.

Step E: Shape the Back Slats

1. Mark the center of the back assembly, 36" (91.44 cm) from the lower edge of the slats. Mark the outside edge of the baluster on each side, 32½" (82.5 cm) from the lower edge. Tack a small nail at each of these marks.

2. Use the nails as reference points to bend a long, flexible straightedge into an arc. Trace that curve onto the slats, then cut along the marked line

C. *Construct the seat frame, using glue and 3" deck screws. Drill counterbored pilot holes and use 2" deck screws to attach the seat slats to the frame.*

D. *Attach the balusters and the back slats to the upper, middle, and lower back braces.*

E. *Trace a graceful curve onto the back slats and trim them to shape, using a jig saw.*

with a jig saw. Sand cut edges smooth with a belt sander.

Step F: Construct the Arms

1. Using the arm template on page 85 and the arm facing template on page 108, trace the appropriate contours onto one arm (M) and one arm facing (N), and use a jig saw to cut them out. Use each as a template to mark and cut the identical (mirrored) shapes on the other arm and arm facing. Chamfer the edges of each piece. On each arm, transfer the placement markings for the arm facings, front and rear arm supports, and back support, as well as for the front chain holes. Drill the front chain holes, using a ⅜" spade bit.

2. Drill pilot holes and attach a front arm support to each arm at the placement marks, using 1½" deck screws.

3. Drill pilot holes and attach the back support (L) to each arm at the placement marks, using four 1½" deck screws.

4. Trim the top of the rear arm supports at a 60° angle. Drill pilot holes and attach a rear arm support to each arm at the placement marks, using 1½" deck screws.

F. *Attach the front arm supports, the rear arm supports, and the back support to the arms.*

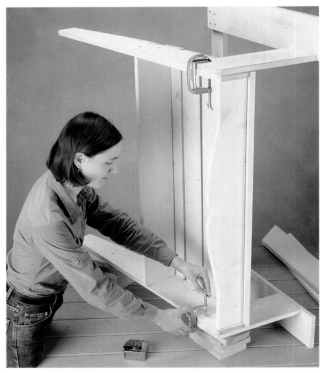

G. *Clamp the seat frame into position and connect it to the arm assembly by driving screws through the seat support and into the front and rear arm supports.*

Step G: Assemble the Seat & Arms

1. Set the seat assembly upright on your work surface, and use scrap lumber to prop it into a stable position. Clamp and prop the arm assembly into position, aligning the arm supports with the placement lines marked on the seat supports. Scribe a cutting line onto each front (0) and rear arm (P) support along the bottoms of the seat supports. Remove the arm assembly and trim the supports along the scribed lines, using a circular saw.

2. Reclamp the arm assembly into position, drill pilot holes, and attach the arm supports to the seat support, using pairs of 1½" deck screws.

3. Drill pilot holes and attach the arm assembly to the seat support by driving pairs of screws through the seat support and into each front arm support from inside the seat frame.

Step H: Attach the Seat Back

1. Position the back so the lower back brace is between the seat supports, flush with their lower edges and aligned with the placement lines. Clamp the back in place. On each side, drill pilot holes and attach the side supports to the lower back brace,

using three 2" deck screws on each side.

2. Drill pilot holes and attach each slat to the back support, using a pair of 1½" deck screws for each.

Step I: Apply Finishing Touches

1. Drill pilot holes and attach the arm facings to the arms and to the front arm supports, using glue and 2" deck screws.

2. Drill pilot holes and attach eye-bolts at marked spots on the seat supports and front arm supports.

3. Lightly sand all cut surfaces and retouch the finish as necessary. Apply a coat of polyurethane sealer to the swing.

4. Hook the chain to the bolts with connecting links and suspend the swing. Adjust the length of the chain and the position of the connection until the swing balances correctly. Mark the position and angle of the chain, then drill ⅜" (15.86 cm) holes through the back of the arms. Thread the chain through the holes and check the balance once again.

5. Hang the swing with heavy screw eyes driven into ceiling joists or into a 2 × 4 lag-screwed across ceiling joists.

H. *Set the back into position and attach the lower back brace to the seat support, then attach the back slats to the back support.*

I. *Install eye-bolts and suspend the swing with a heavy chain. Adjust the chain until the swing is balanced, then mark and drill the rear chain holes in the arms.*

Stained Glass Planter

Hypertufa—mainly a mixture of portland cement, peat moss, and perlite—is a wonderful medium for building all sorts of garden accents. It's as durable as concrete but without the weight. You can mold it into almost anything for which you can build a form.

While researching a book on garden-style decorating, we came across a poured-concrete planter that had a stained glass design embedded in it. It was beautiful, but it was also extreme—extremely heavy and extremely expensive. We did a little experimenting and were delighted to find that stained glass could be embedded in our old favorite, hypertufa.

You have to be fairly careful as you pack the hypertufa around the stained glass. We tried several methods of holding the glass to the sides of the form, but found that double-stick carpet tape works best. Although it releases easily when the forms are removed, it holds the glass quite securely during the forming process.

It's important to tamp the hypertufa consistently throughout. Loosely packed hypertufa has many voids and air pockets, which are not especially attractive. Firmly packed hypertufa has an even, consistent, more appealing surface.

This project is fairly basic. Once you have some experience with these techniques, use your imagination and taste to adapt the basic project and create planters tailored to your personal style and your garden.

TOOLS & MATERIALS

- Glass cutter
- Breaker pliers
- Rotary tool or Carborundum stone
- Jig saw
- Straightedge
- Drill
- Hacksaw
- Wheelbarrow or mixing trough
- Hammer
- Chisel
- Paint scraper
- Wire brush
- Fine wire mesh
- Stained glass (two colors)

- 2"-thick (5 cm) polystyrene insulation board
- 3½" (8.9 cm) deck screws (40)
- Duct tape
- Double-stick carpet tape
- Scrap of 4"-dia. (10 cm) PVC pipe
- Dust mask
- Gloves
- Portland cement
- Peat moss
- Perlite
- Concrete reinforcing fibers
- Concrete dye (optional)
- Plastic tarp
- Scrap 2 × 4 (5 × 10 cm)

CUTTING LIST

Outer Form			Inner Form		
Floor	1	22" × 32" (56 × 81 cm)	Sides	2	7" × 24" (18 × 61 cm)
Sides	2	11" × 32" (28 × 81 cm)	Ends & Center Support		
Ends	2	11" × 18" (28 × 46 cm)		3	7" × 10" (18 × 25 cm)

ASSEMBLED FORMS

OUTER FORM

Floor
22 × 32"
(55.88 × 81.28 cm)

End 11 × 18"
(27.94 × 45.72 cm)

Side 11 × 32"
(27.94 × 81.28 cm)

3 × 4"
(5 × 10 cm) PVC
pipe (to create
weep holes)

INNER FORM

End 7 × 10"
(18 × 25 cm)

Center support
7 × 10"
(17.8 × 25.4 cm)

Side 7 × 24"
(17.8 × 61 cm)

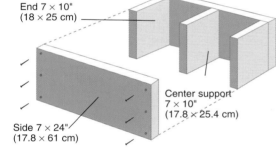

2" (5 cm)   2" (5 cm)

HOW TO BUILD A STAINED GLASS PLANTER
Step A: Make the Pattern and Cut the Glass

1. Mark twelve 2" (5 cm) squares onto one piece of the stained glass. Divide each square into two equal triangles.

2. Mark twenty-two 2" squares onto the second piece of stained glass.

3. Score the glass along the marked lines, using a glass cutter. Extend the score from one side of the glass to the other. Hold breaker pliers next to the score, and snap the glass apart. File the edges of each piece with a rotary tool or a Carborundum stone; rinse and dry each piece.

Step B: Build the Forms

1. Measure, mark, and cut pieces of 2"-thick polystyrene insulation board to the dimensions in the cutting list, using a jig saw.

2. Construct the inner form: Fit an end piece between the two side pieces and fasten each joint, using three 3½" deck screws. Repeat to fasten the other end and to add the center support. Wrap duct tape around the form at each joint.

3. Construct the outer form: Use deck screws and duct tape, as with the inner form. Set the bottom piece squarely on top of the resulting rectangle, and then screw and tape it securely in place.

4. Cut two 3" (7.6 cm) pieces of 4"-dia. PVC pipe, using a hacksaw, and set them aside.

Step C: Form the Floor

1. Center the pieces of PVC pipe in the floor of the outer form and press them into the foam, but not through the foam; these pipes establish the planter's drainage holes.

2. Mix the hypertufa, following the directions on pages 106 to 107. Be sure to wear a dust mask and gloves when handling dry cement mix; also wear gloves when working with wet cement.

3. Pack hypertufa onto the floor of the form, pressing down firmly and packing it tightly around the pieces of PVC. Continue adding hypertufa until you've created a solid, 2"-thick (5 cm) floor. (Be careful not to get hypertufa inside the PVC pipe.)

Step D: Build the Walls

1. Attach double-stick carpet tape 2" from the top edge on the inside of the side and end pieces of the outer form. Remove the tape's backing, exposing the adhesive.

2. Arrange the stained glass pieces on the tape, positioned as planned for the design.

3. Center the inner form within the outer form. Add hypertufa between the forms. Using your gloved hands, pack it firmly. Make sure the walls will be solid—they need to withstand the weight and pressure of soil, moisture, and growing plants. Continue adding hypertufa until it reaches the top of the forms.

Step E: Allow to Dry & Remove the Forms

1. Cover the planter with a plastic tarp, and let it dry for two to three days. If the weather is extremely warm, remove the tarp and mist the planter with water occasionally during the curing process.

2. Remove the tape and screws from the outer form, and pull the polystyrene away from the planter. Work carefully so the form can be reused, if desired. If the walls appear to be dry enough to be

A. *Mark, score, and cut triangles and squares from stained glass.*

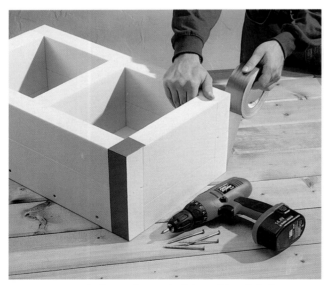

B. *To construct the forms, fasten the joints with 3½" deck screws; then reinforce them with duct tape.*

C. *Pack hypertufa onto the floor of the form; press it down firmly to create a level, 2"-thick floor.*

handled, remove the inner forms. If not, let the planter cure for another day or two, and then remove the inner form.

Step F: Complete the Curing Process

1. If you want to give the planter a rustic appearance, this is the time to create it. Working carefully with a hammer and chisel, knock off the corners and sharp edges.

2. Next, add texture to the sides by using a paint scraper or screwdriver to scrape grooves into the hypertufa.

3. Finally, brush the surface with a wire brush. Avoid the areas immediately surrounding the stained glass, but be bold in other areas. The more texture you create, the more time-worn the planter will appear to be.

4. Cover the planter with plastic, and let it cure for about a month. Uncover it at least once a week, and mist it with water to slow down the curing process. Although it's natural to be impatient, don't rush this step. The more slowly the hypertufa cures, the stronger and more durable the planter will be.

5. Unwrap the planter and let it cure outside, uncovered, for several weeks. Periodically wash it down with water, inside and out, to remove the alkaline residue of the concrete (which would otherwise endanger plants grown in the container). Adding vinegar to the water speeds this process somewhat, but it still takes several weeks. Again, this step is important, so don't rush it.

6. After the planter has cured outside for several weeks, put it inside, away from any sources of moisture, to cure for several more weeks.

Note: Before filling the planter with potting soil, cover the drainage holes with fine wire mesh.

D. *Center the inner form within the walls of the outer form. Pack hypertufa between the forms to create the planter's walls.*

E. *After the planter has dried for two to three days, remove the screws and carefully disassemble the forms.*

F. *Round the corners and texture the surface of the planter with a hammer and chisel, paint scraper, and wire brush. Work carefully so you don't dislodge the stained glass.*

Copper Gate

This copper gate is an example of how ordinary materials can be used in surprising ways. A wonderful accent for a garden entry, it's nothing more than simple combinations of copper pipe and fittings and a few pieces of inexpensive hardware. Although it's sturdy and fully operational, it isn't meant to provide security or to handle a constant flow of traffic. Set into a living wall or a section of fence where it receives light use, it can provide decades of service.

The finish can be protected to maintain the bright color or allowed to develop a patina. To maintain the original color, spray the new copper with an acrylic sealer. On the other hand, if you don't want to wait for the patina to develop on its own, rub the finished piece with the cut face of a lemon or a tomato—the acid will speed the chemical process that creates the patina.

We used a copper watering can for an accent piece, but there's really no limit to what you could choose. If an object appeals to you and can be wired or soldered securely into place, you can make it work. You may have to adjust the dimensions of the display frame, but that's a simple matter of making a few calculations before you begin cutting the copper.

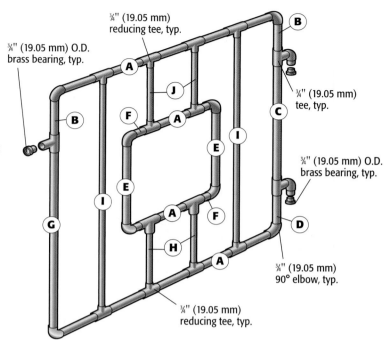

¾" (19.05 mm) reducing tee, typ.

¾" (19.05 mm) O.D. brass bearing, typ.

¾" (19.05 mm) tee, typ.

¾" (19.05 mm) O.D. brass bearing, typ.

¾" (19.05 mm) 90° elbow, typ.

¾" (19.05 mm) reducing tee, typ.

TOOLS & MATERIALS

- Bandsaw or tubing cutter
- Paintbrush
- 4-ft. (1.22 m) level
- Reciprocating saw or hand saw
- Locking pliers or pipe wrench
- Drill and ½" (12.7 mm) spade bit
- Power auger or posthole digger
- Shovel
- Mason's trowel
- Propane torch
- Emery cloth
- Wire brush
- Flux and flux brush
- Solder
- 4 × 4 (10 × 10 cm) posts, 8 ft. (2.44 m) (2)
- Paint, stain, or sealer
- Deck post cap and finial (2)
- ¾" (19.05 mm) copper pipe, 20 ft. (6 m)

- ½" (12.7 mm) copper pipe, 10 ft. (3 m)
- ⅜" (9.5 mm) flexible copper tubing (18" [45.72 cm])
- ⅝ × ¾ × 1 (15.86 × 19.05 × 2.54 cm) brass flange bearings (3)
- ¾" (19.05 mm) 90° elbows (10)
- ¾ to ½" (19.05 to 12.7 mm) reducing tees (12)
- ¾" (19.05 mm) tees (3)
- Lag screwhinges for chain link fence (2)
- Coarse gravel
- Concrete mix
- 8-gauge (4 mm) copper wire (about 8" [20.32 cm])
- Copper watering can
- 16-gauge (1.5 mm) copper wire (about 24" [61 cm])
- Galvanized finishing nails

CUTTING LIST

Key	Part	Size	Number
A	¾" (19 mm) pipe	6½" (16.5 cm)	12
B	¾" pipe	6" (15.25 cm)	2
C	¾" pipe	23¾" (60.33 cm)	1
D	¾" pipe	5" (12.7 cm)	1
E	¾" pipe	12½" (31.75 cm)	2
F	¾" pipe	2½" (6.35 cm)	4
G	¾" pipe	29½" (74.93 cm)	1
H	½" (12.7 mm) pipe	10" (25.4 cm)	2
I	½" pipe	36¾" (93.35 cm)	2
J	½" pipe	12¼" (31.11 cm)	2

HOW TO BUILD A COPPER GATE

Step A: Cut the Copper Parts

1. Measure and mark the pipe, according to the cutting list and diagram at right.

2. Cut the copper pipe to length, using a bandsaw or tubing cutter. Sand the ends of all the pipes with emery cloth, and scour the insides of the fittings with a wire brush. Apply flux to all the mating surfaces.

A. *Measure, mark, and cut the copper pipe, using a tubing cutter. Clean and flux the pipe and fittings.*

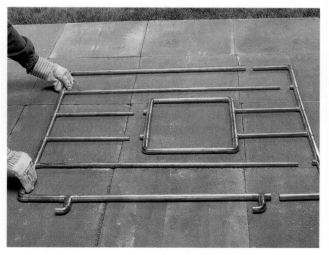

B. *Dry-fit the bottom assembly of the gate, and then the top assembly. Connect the two assemblies.*

Step B: Assemble the Gate Pieces

1. Dry-fit the pieces of the top of the gate and the display frame, referring to the diagram on page 95.

2. Assemble the bottom run of the gate, again referring to the diagram as necessary.

3. Join the top and bottom sections of the gate. Measure from one corner of the gate to the diagonally opposite corner. Repeat at the opposite corners. Adjust the pieces until these measurements are equal, which indicates that the gate is square.

Step C: Solder the Joints & Add the Bushings

1. Solder each joint, beginning at the bottom of the gate and working toward the top.

2. At each of the hinge extensions and at the latch extension, add a brass flange bearing. As you solder these bearings in place, direct the torch's flame more toward the bearing than toward the elbow—brass heats more slowly than copper.

Step D: Install & Mark the Gate Posts

1. Paint, stain, or seal the posts.

2. Mark the post positions 49½" (1.26 m) apart on center. Dig postholes, using a power auger or posthole digger. Make each hole 6" (15.25 cm) deeper than the post footing depth specified by local building code and about twice the width of the post. Pour a 6" (15.25 cm) layer of gravel into each hole.

3. Position the posts. Check each for plumb and adjust as necessary, maintaining the spacing between them as accurately as possible. Brace each post with scrap 2 × 4s (5 × 10 cm) secured to adjacent sides.

4. Mix concrete and fill the holes, overfilling each slightly. Shape the concrete around the bottom of

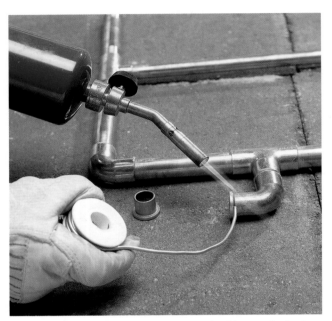

C. *Solder the joints of the gate. Add brass bushings to the latch and hinge extensions and solder them in place.*

D. *Install the gate posts, then position the gate and mark the locations for the latch and for the hinge extensions.*

E. *Drill pilot holes at the marked locations on the hinge-side post. Drive a lag screwhinge into each pilot hole. Make sure the hinge pin is facing up when the screwhinge is in position.*

the post to form a rounded crown that will shed water. Let the concrete cure for 2 days, then remove the braces.

5. On the first post, measure and mark a point 47½" (121 cm) from the ground. Using a level, draw a line across the post at the mark, then across the opposite post. Trim the posts, using a reciprocating saw or hand saw. Paint, stain, or seal the cut ends.

6. Set a deck post cap and finial on top of each post and nail it in place, using galvanized finish nails.

7. Cut two 4¼" (10.8 cm) spacers. Center the gate between the posts, resting it on the spacers. Mark the hinge-side post to indicate the locations of the hinge extensions. Mark the latch-side post to indicate the location of the latch extension.

Step E: Install the Lag Screws for the Hinges

1. At each of the marked locations on the hinge-side post, drill a ½" (12.7 mm) pilot hole approximately 2¾" (6.9 cm) into the post. Drill these holes carefully—they must be as straight as possible.

2. Drive a lag screwhinge into each pilot hole, using a locking pliers or pipe wrench to twist it into place. The hinge pin needs to be facing up when the lag screw is in its final position.

Step F: Add the Latch

1. At the marked location on the latch-side post, drill a ½" hole straight through the post.

2. Cut 15" (38.1 cm) to 18" (45.72 cm) of ⅜" flexible copper. Drill a hole through the tubing, 2½" (6.35 cm) from one end. At the opposite end, form a decorative coil. Cut a 2" (5 cm) piece of 8-gauge copper wire and form a decorative coil at one end.

3. Insert the latch through the hole in the latch-side post. Thread the wire through the hole in the tubing, then create a small loop below the tubing. This wire loop keeps the latch from falling out of the post.

Step G: Hang the Watering Can

1. Position the watering can within the display frame on the gate. Mark the spots where the handle and spout will meet the copper pipe; clean and flux those areas. Wrap 16-gauge copper wire around the handle of the watering can, using 6 or 8 wraps of wire to connect it to the display frame in the marked spot. Add a little more flux, then solder the handle to the frame. The flux will draw the solder into the crevices between the wire wraps to create a strong, solid joint.

2. Thread a piece of 16-gauge copper wire through a hole in the watering can's spout. Wrap the other end around the frame at the marked location. Flux and solder the wire wrap as described above.

F. *Drill a hole on one end of a piece of flexible copper. At the opposite end, bend a coil. Insert the tubing through a hole in the latch-side post, and thread a loop of wire through the hole in the tubing.*

G. *Set the watering can into position and secure it, using 16-gauge wire. Solder the wrapped wire to the gate frame.*

Pipe Pergola

When I first saw the movie, *Chocolat*, my favorite element wasn't the plot or the character development or even the cinematography. It was the cloth-draped pergola under which a very special birthday dinner was served. I couldn't wait for the movie to come out on video so I could stop the tape, study the pergola, and figure out how to build it.

And that's exactly what we did. When we tried to use threaded galvanized pipe and standard fittings, it quickly became a complicated process. That's when I learned about these quick-set fittings manufactured by Grainger. Using these fittings, there's no need to thread the pipe, which simplifies things enormously. It also means you can use either galvanized plumbing pipe or electrical conduit, which is

lighter and less expensive. (We used conduit.)

We ordered the fittings directly from a Grainger distributor, which we located in the phone directory. You can also find the company on-line at www.grainger.com or by phone, toll-free at 1-888-285-5700.

We designed our pergola to accommodate a small patio table, but if you have a larger table or want more room, you could use longer pipes and/or add another section to the pergola.

TOOLS & MATERIALS

- Sewing machine
- Scissors
- Hacksaw
- 26 × 86" (66.04 cm × 2.29 m) fabric (3)
- 1½" (3.8 cm) conduit
- 1½" (3.8 cm) quick-set pipe fittings:
    4 side outlet elbows
    6 single socket tees
- Allen wrench
- Base flanges (4)
- Shovel
- 1-gallon (4 l) paint cans (4)
- Sand
- Quick-setting cement
- Level
- Hand tamp

CUTTING LIST

Part	No.	Size
Cross braces	3	72" (1.83 m)
Side braces	4	72" (1.83 m)
Legs	4	96" (2.44 m)

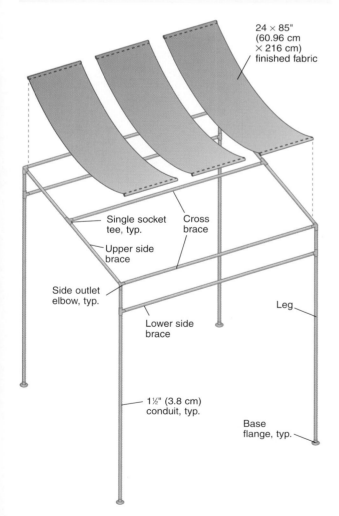

24 × 85"
(60.96 cm
× 216 cm)
finished fabric

Single socket tee, typ.

Cross brace

Upper side brace

Side outlet elbow, typ.

Lower side brace

Leg

1½" (3.8 cm) conduit, typ.

Base flange, typ.

HOW TO BUILD A PIPE PERGOLA
Step A: Prepare the Fabric

1. Cut three 28 × 90" (71.12 cm × 2.29 m) pieces of fabric. Along each side of each strip, turn under ½" and then repeat to form a double-fold hem. Sew along the edge, using a straight stitch.

2. On each strip, fold under ½" at one end, then fold under 1½" (3.8 cm). Sew close to the first fold, forming a rod pocket. Repeat to form a pocket at the opposite end of each strip.

A. Cut and hem three strips of fabric for the sunshade. Form a rod pocket at each end of each strip.

Step B: Prepare the Cross Braces

1. Cut the cross braces and side braces from 1½" conduit, using a hacksaw.

2. Slide one cross brace through the pockets of the three prepared fabric strips. Slide another cross brace through the pockets at the opposite end of the strips. Put one side outlet elbow on each end of these cross braces. Tighten the set screws just enough to hold the elbows in place.

Step C: Assemble the Roof

1. On two 72" side braces, mark a line 38" (96.52 cm) from one end. Position a single socket tee at each mark, and tighten the set screws just enough to hold the tees in place.

2. Position a cross brace between each set of side outlet elbows, and one cross brace between the single socket tees on the upper side braces. Gently tighten the set screws on the fittings, using an allen wrench.

Step D: Construct the Leg Assemblies

1. Mark a line 12" (30.5 cm) from one end of each of the four 96" pieces of 1½" conduit that are the legs.

2. On each leg, position a single socket tee at the 12" line, and add a base flange to the opposite end.

3. Position a lower side brace in the tees between pairs of legs and gently tighten the set screws.

4. Prop the roof into position and connect the leg assemblies to the roof assembly at the side outlet elbows.

Step E: Install the Pergola

1. Stake the locations for the pergola's legs. At each stake, dig a hole about 1" (2.54 cm) deeper than a 1-gallon paint can. Check the holes as you go; keep the sides straight and the bottoms as level as possible. Add a 1"-layer of sand to each hole.

2. Put one paint can in each hole. Set the pergola into position, with each leg centered in a can. Mix quick-setting cement and fill the cans. Let the cement dry, according to manufacturer's directions.

3. Check the various parts of the pergola to make sure everything is level and plumb. If necessary, add sand beneath the cans or adjust the fittings at the joints. When you're satisfied, completely tighten each fitting.

4. Fill in the holes, tamping the soil firmly around the cans.

B. *Cut the cross braces and slide the fabric panels onto them.*

C. *Join the roof pieces with single socket tees. Tighten the fittings, using an allen wrench.*

D. *Construct the leg assemblies and add them to the cross braces.*

E. *Set the legs in buckets filled with quick-setting cement. Adjust and level as necessary.*

TIP: FASTEN THE PERGOLA TO A DECK OR PATIO

If you prefer to fasten the pergola directly to a deck or patio, it's a simple matter. For a deck, position the pergola and mark the holes of the base flanges. Drill pilot holes, then use galvanized deck screws to fasten the base flanges to the deck.

You can fasten the pergola to a patio in much the same way, but use a carbide-tipped masonry bit to drill the pilot holes and masonry screws to attach the base flanges to the patio.

TIP: TRAIN ROSES ONTO THE PERGOLA

Training roses onto a pergola is another memorable way to produce a shady dining spot.

To adapt the pergola to this purpose, you'll need concrete reinforcing mesh, bolt cutters, needlenose pliers, and 14-gauge (2 mm) copper wire.

Omit the fabric described on page 99. Cut the reinforcing mesh to fit the top of the pergola, using bolt cutters. If necessary, join sections with twisted pieces of 14-gauge wire. Wrap the ends of the mesh around the cross braces of the pergola, then secure it with twists of wire placed every 3 to 4" (7.6 to 10 cm) around the perimeter.

You'll get the best results with climber, rambler, or pillar roses. Because roses don't have holdfasts or tendrils like climbing vines, they need to be supported in order to grow on vertical surfaces.

Plant the rose bush near the pergola and let it grow. When the canes are long enough, begin training them. You'll need protective gloves, plant tape, and a pair of garden scissors. Arch a cane, putting it under tension and bringing its end lower than its middle. (When the end is lower than the middle, buds along the cane develop and produce lateral shoots that bear blooms.) Securely tie the cane's end and center to the support, using plant tape. Bend remaining canes along the supports and tie them in place. Spread alternating canes to the left and right, covering the pergola.

After a week or two, the canes will be adjusted to their new positions and you can add ties along the length of each.

Basic Techniques

As we were designing projects and deciding how to describe construction processes, our main goal was to make sure that average people could follow the directions, master the techniques, and successfully complete any project in this book. As you look through its pages, we hope you'll see ideas that inspire you and information that gives you confidence.

Most of the projects use ordinary materials and common techniques. Still, you may need an introduction to basic skills, such as soldering or working with hypertufa. Especially if you haven't soldered before, you might want to practice with scraps before you begin a project.

If you have questions after reading through the instructions and the background for the techniques required, you have a couple of options. First, most hardware stores and home centers have staff members who are happy to answer questions. Many home centers have information desks, and some even have classes on techniques such as soldering. When you buy materials, ask for help or additional information.

If you're still having trouble, contact us. You can reach us at Creative Publishing international, 5900 Green Oak Drive, Minnetonka, MN 55343 or at DIY@creativepub.com. Tim and I love to hear from people who are bringing our ideas to life, and we especially love to see pictures of your creations.

We hope you have as much fun building these garden accents as we've had creating them.

IN THIS CHAPTER:

Cutting & Soldering Copper

A soldered pipe joint, also called a sweated joint, is made by heating a copper or brass fitting with a propane torch until the fitting is just hot enough to melt solder. The heat then draws the solder into the gap between the fitting and the copper pipe, forming a strong seal.

Using too much heat is the most common mistake made by beginners. To avoid this error, remember that the tip of the torch's inner flame produces the most heat. Direct the flame carefully—solder will flow in the direction the heat has traveled. Heat the pipe just until the flux sizzles; remove the flame and touch the solder to the pipe. The heated pipe will quickly melt the solder.

Soldering copper pipe and fittings isn't difficult, but it requires some patience and skill. It's a good idea to practice soldering pieces of scrap pipe before taking on a large project.

HOW TO SOLDER COPPER PIPE
Step A: Cut the Pipe

1. Measure and mark the pipe. Place a tubing cutter over the pipe with the cutting wheel centered over the marked line. Tighten the handle until the pipe rests on both rollers.

2. Turn the tubing cutter one rotation to score a continuous line around the pipe. Then rotate the cutter in the opposite direction. After every two rotations, tighten the handle. Rotate the cutter until the pipe separates.

Step B: Clean the Pipe & Fittings

To form a good seal with solder, the ends of all pipes and the insides of all fittings must be free of dirt and grease. Remove metal burrs from the inside edge of the cut pipe, using the reaming point on the tubing cutter or a round file. Sand the ends of pipes with emery cloth, and scour the insides of the fittings with a wire brush.

Step C: Flux & Dry-fit the Pipes

1. Apply a thin layer of water-soluble paste flux to the end of each pipe, using a flux brush. The flux should cover about 1" (2.54 cm) of the end of the pipe.

2. Insert the pipe into the fitting until the pipe is tight against the fitting socket, and twist the fitting slightly to spread the flux. If a series of pipes and fittings (a run) is involved, flux and dry-fit the entire run without soldering any of the joints. When you're sure the run is correctly assembled and everything fits, take it apart and prepare to solder the joints.

Step D: Heat the Fittings

1. Shield flammable work surfaces from the heat of the torch. Although heat-absorbent pads are available

A. *Position the tubing cutter, and score a line around the pipe. Rotate the cutter until the pipe separates.*

B. *Clean inside the fittings with a wire brush, and deburr the pipes with the reaming point on the tubing cutter.*

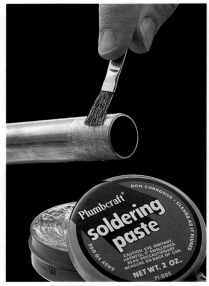

C. *Brush a thin layer of flux onto the end of each pipe. Assemble the joint, twisting the fitting to spread the flux.*

for this purpose, you can use a double layer of 26-gauge (0.55 mm) sheet metal. The reflective quality of the sheet metal helps joints heat evenly.

2. Unwind 8" (20 cm) to 10" (25 cm) of solder from the spool. To make it easier to maneuver the solder all the way around a joint, bend the first 2" (5 cm) of the wire solder to a 90° angle.

3. Open the gas valve and light the propane torch. Adjust the valve until the inner portion of the flame is 1" to 2" long.

4. Hold the tip of the flame against the middle of the fitting for 4 to 5 seconds or until the flux begins to sizzle. Heat the other side of the joint, distributing the heat evenly. Move the flame around the joint in the direction the solder should flow. Touch the solder to the pipe, just below the fitting. If it melts, the joint is hot enough.

Step E: Apply the Solder

Quickly apply solder along both seams of the fitting, allowing capillary action to draw the liquified solder into the fitting. When the joint is filled, solder begins to form droplets on the bottom. A correctly soldered joint shows a thin bead of silver-colored solder around the lip of the fitting. It typically takes about ½" (12 mm) of solder wire to fill a joint in ½" pipe.

If the solder pools around the fitting rather than filling the joint as it cools, reheat the area until the solder liquifies and is drawn in slightly.

Note: Always turn off the propane torch immediately after you've finished soldering; make sure the gas valve is completely closed.

Step F: Wipe Away Excess Solder & Check the Joint

1. Let the joint sit undisturbed until the solder loses its shiny color. Don't touch it before then—the copper will be quite hot.

2. When the joint is cool enough to touch, wipe away excess flux and solder, using a clean, dry rag. When the joint is completely cool, check for gaps around the edges. If you find gaps, apply more flux to the rim of the joint and resolder it.

3. If, for some reason, you need to take apart a soldered joint, you can reverse the process. First, light the torch and heat the fitting until the solder becomes shiny and begins to melt. Then use channel-type pliers to separate the pipe from the fitting. To remove the old solder, heat the ends of the pipe, and use a dry rag to carefully wipe away the melted solder. When the pipe is cool, polish the ends down to bare metal, using emery cloth. Discard the old fittings—they can't be reused.

D. *Heat the fitting until the flux begins to sizzle. Concentrate the tip of the torch's flame on the middle of the fitting.*

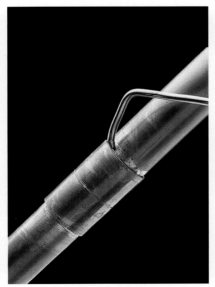

E. *Push ½" to ¾" of solder into each joint, allowing capillary action to draw liquified solder into the joint.*

F. *When the joint has cooled, wipe away excess solder with a dry rag. Be careful: The pipes will be hot.*

Working with Hypertufa

Hypertufa is wonderfully suited to building garden ornaments. There are many recipes available, and some are more reliable than others. Experience leads me to prefer these two recipes. Recipe #1, which contains fiberglass fibers, is ideal for producing lightweight, durable, medium-to-large planting containers. Recipe #2, which contains sand, is especially appropriate for smaller items and those that must hold water.

The ingredients for both recipes are widely available at home and garden centers. Use portland cement rather than a prepared cement mix that contains gravel (which contributes unnecessary weight and gives the finished container a coarse texture). In Recipe #1, perlite, a soil lightener, takes the place of the aggregate typically found in concrete. For Recipe #2, use fine-textured mason's sand—it produces a stronger container than coarser grades of sand.

Peat moss naturally includes a range of textures, some of which are too coarse for hypertufa. Sifting

---

HYPERTUFA RECIPES

Recipe #1

2 buckets portland cement
3 buckets sifted peat moss
3 buckets perlite
1 handful of fiberglass fibers
powdered cement dye (optional)

Recipe #2

3 buckets portland cement
3 buckets sand
3 buckets sifted peat moss

---

the peat moss through hardware cloth takes care of that problem. If you plan to make several hypertufa pieces, it's most efficient to buy a large bale of peat moss, sift the entire bale, then store the sifted material for use over time.

The fiberglass fibers in Recipe #1 contribute strength to the mixture. This product is available at most building centers, but if you have trouble locating it, try a concrete or masonry supply center.

Hypertufa dries to the color of concrete. If you prefer another color, simply add a powdered concrete dye during the mixing process. Tinting products are very effective, so start with a small amount and add more if necessary.

HOW TO MAKE HYPERTUFA
Step A: Sift the Peat Moss & Build the Forms

1. Place the hardware cloth across a large bucket or wheelbarrow. Rub the peat moss across the hardware cloth, sifting it through the mesh. Discard any debris or large particles.

The materials for making hypertufa are inexpensive and widely available. They include portland cement, perlite, peat moss, fiberglass fibers, mason's sand, concrete dye, hardware cloth, a plastic tarp, a dust mask, and gloves.

A. *Sift the peat moss through hardware cloth to remove any debris or large particles and break up clumps.*

2. Build forms from 2" (5 cm) polystyrene insulation (see individual projects). Secure joints with 2½" (6.35 cm) deck screws, and reinforce them with duct tape or gaffer's tape. If the piece is a planting container, be sure to provide adequate drainage holes.

Step B: Mix the Ingredients

1. Measure the cement, peat moss, and perlite or sand, and add them to a mixing trough or wheelbarrow. Using a hoe or small shovel, blend these ingredients thoroughly. If you're using Recipe #1, add the fiberglass fibers and mix again. Add concrete dye, if desired, and mix until the fiberglass fibers and the dye powder are evenly distributed throughout.

2. Add water and blend thoroughly. The amount of water required varies, so add a little at a time. It's easy to add more, but very difficult to correct the situation after you've added too much. The hypertufa is ready to be molded when you can squeeze a few drops of water from a handful.

Step C: Form the Hypertufa

1. Pack the hypertufa into the form and firmly tamp it down. Continue adding and tamping until hypertufa reaches the recommended depth or fills the form (see individual projects).

2. Cover the project with plastic, and let it dry for 48 hours.

3. Disassemble the forms and remove the piece.

Step D: Shape & Cure the Piece

1. Sculpt the appearance of the piece by knocking off the corners and sharp edges. Add texture to the sides of the piece by using a paint scraper or screwdriver to scrape grooves into them. Finally, brush the surface with a wire brush.

2. Wrap the piece in plastic, and put it in a cool place to cure for about a month. Remember, the longer the hypertufa cures, the stronger it will be.

3. Unwrap the piece and let it cure outside, uncovered. If you're building a planter, let it cure for several weeks, periodically rinsing it with water to remove some of the alkalinity, which could harm plants that are grown in the container. Adding vinegar to the rinse water speeds this process.

After the planter has cured outside for several weeks, move it inside, away from any sources of moisture, to cure for another week or so.

4. The fiberglass fibers in Recipe #1 produce a hairy fringe. Make sure pieces made from this recipe are dry, and then use a propane torch to burn off the fringe. Move the torch quickly, holding it in each spot no more than a second or two. If pockets of moisture remain, they may get hot enough to explode, leaving pot holes in the piece.

5. Apply a coat of masonry sealer to basins or other pieces that must hold water.

B. *Measure the ingredients into a mixing container and blend thoroughly. Add water, a little at a time, and mix.*

C. *Pack the hypertufa into the forms, and tamp it firmly. Cover the project with plastic, and let it cure for 48 hours.*

D. *Let the piece cure. Rinse it repeatedly; let it dry completely. Use a propane torch to burn off any fiberglass fibers.*

Patterns

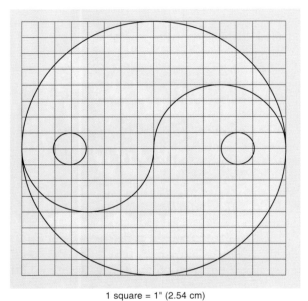

1 square = 1" (2.54 cm)

YIN/YANG FOUNTAIN DESIGN

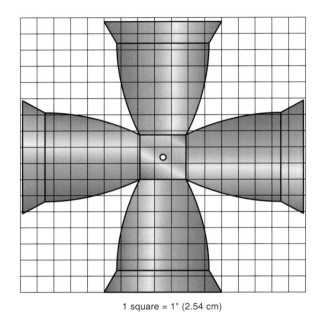

1 square = 1" (2.54 cm)

**DECORATIVE BIRDHOUSE
ROOF DETAIL**

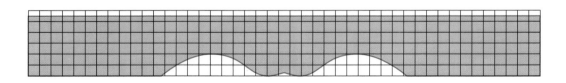

1 square = 1" (2.54 cm)

**BIRDHOUSE PLANT STAND
SKIRTING FRONT DETAIL**

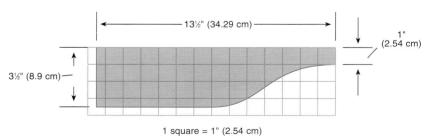

1 square = 1" (2.54 cm)

**PORCH SWING
ARM FACING DETAIL**

Index

Index continued

Also from

CREATIVE PUBLISHING INTERNATIONAL

Garden Style

*I*n growing numbers, dedicated gardeners are embracing their favorite activity as more than a hobby–it's becoming a lifestyle choice. Garden Style shows how to apply this exciting trend to living spaces throughout the home. From shutters and window boxes hung on interior walls to a charming headboard that mimics a garden wall, this book features hundreds of ideas and dozens of stylish functional projects. Each project can be completed in a a few steps, following the simple directions provided.

ISBN 1-58923-007-8 . . . .$19.95

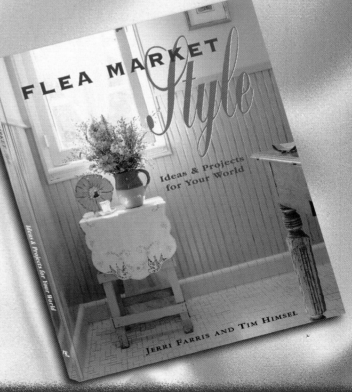

Flea Market Style

*T*his book features hundreds of ideas and dozens of projects for transforming flea market finds into reclaimed treasure. In some cases, it's simply a matter of finding the right setting for an object with an interesting shape, color, or texture. In others, a few inspired alterations create a whole new life in an entirely different role–an old panel door becomes a mirrored plant stand, for example. Flea Market Style gives readers complete instructions for creating dozens of simple but ingenious projects.

ISBN 1-58923-000-0 . . . .$19.95

CREATIVE PUBLISHING INTERNATIONAL

5900 Green Oak Drive
Minnetonka, MN 55343

www.creativepub.com

Also from

CREATIVE PUBLISHING INTERNATIONAL

Basic Wiring & Electrical Repairs
Advanced Home Wiring
Home Plumbing Projects & Repairs
Advanced Home Plumbing
Carpentry: Remodeling
Remodeling Kitchens
Bathroom Remodeling
Flooring Projects & Techniques
Easy Wood Furniture Projects
Built-In Projects for the Home
Decorating With Paint & Wallcovering
Refinishing & Finishing Wood
Designing Your Outdoor Home
Building Your Outdoor Home
Fences, Walls & Gates
Building Decks
Great Decks & Furnishings
Advanced Deck Building
Building Porches & Patios
Exterior Home Repairs & Improvements
Outdoor Wood Furnishings
Home Masonry Repairs & Projects
Stonework & Masonry Projects
Finishing Basements & Attics
Complete Guide to Painting & Decorating
Complete Guide to Home Plumbing
Complete Guide to Home Wiring
Complete Guide to Home Storage
Complete Guide to Building Decks
Complete Guide to Home Carpentry
Complete Photo Guide to Home Repair
Complete Photo Guide to Home Improvement
Complete Photo Guide to Outdoor Home Improvement

ISBN 0-86573-579-4 $24.95

ISBN 0-86573-590-5 $14.95

ISBN 0-86573-727-4 $14.95

CREATIVE PUBLISHING INTERNATIONAL

5900 GREEN OAK DRIVE
MINNETONKA, MN 55343

WWW.CREATIVEPUB.COM